David Lynch

Director David Lynch is best known for films that channel the uncanny and the weird into a distinct "Lynchian" aesthetic, in which sound and music play a key role: Lynch not only writes his intended sounds into the script but also often takes on the role of creating the sounds himself. This concise study explores what makes Lynch's sonic imprint distinct, breaking down three different sound styles that create Lynch's sound aesthetic across his films. Showing how sound offers new insights into the aesthetic and narrative work of Lynch's filmmaking, this book highlights new dimensions in the work of a key American auteur and deconstructs the process of building a unique sound world.

Reba Wissner is Assistant Professor of Musicology at Columbus State University.

Filmmakers and Their Soundtracks

Series Editor: James Wierzbicki, *The University of Sydney, Australia*

Terrence Malick
Sonic Style
James Wierzbicki

Howard Hawks
Music as Communication in Film
Gregory Camp

Music and Sound in the Worlds of Michel Gondry
Kate McQuiston

Music and Sound in the Films of Dennis Hopper
Stephen Lee Naish

David Lynch
Sonic Style
Reba Wissner

For more information about this series, please visit: www.routledge.com/Filmmakers-and-Their-Soundtracks/book-series/FILMSNDTRCK

David Lynch

Sonic Style

Reba Wissner

NEW YORK AND LONDON

First published 2024
by Routledge
605 Third Avenue, New York, NY 10158

and by Routledge
4 Park Square, Milton Park, Abingdon, Oxon, OX14 4RN

Routledge is an imprint of the Taylor & Francis Group, an informa business

ISBN: 9781032208343 (hbk)
ISBN: 9781032208350 (pbk)
ISBN: 9781003265450 (ebk)

DOI: 10.4324/9781003265450

Typeset in Times New Roman
by Deanta Global Publishing Services, Chennai, India

To Tommy and Lizzy, forever my babies.

Contents

Acknowledgments

There are many people who I have to thank for making this book possible. First, series editor James Wierzbicki was constantly supportive and patient with this project and Genevieve Aoki also exhibited patience beyond what I could ever ask. My graduate assistant, Naomi Israel, helped with getting the volume into its final form. I am grateful that I got to speak with three Lynch collaborators who gave me insight into their work with the director: Angelo Badalamenti, Dean Hurley, and Marek Zebrowski, the latter of whom also supplied me with photographs of he and Lynch collaborating together. Special thanks go out to Lisa Cooper Vest for connecting me with Zebrowski and for W. David Lichty, who connected me to Tim Grieving, who then connected me with Badalamenti.

My parents were endlessly supportive throughout this project, even if they didn't quite understand Lynch's works. My dogs, Tommy and Lizzy, were amazing companions and kept me grounded when things got rough. My dear friends and collaborators, Kate Galloway, Jessica Getman, and Katherine Reed were my support system, and Katie, as my co-editor of *The Music in Twin Peaks: Listen to the Sounds*, entertained many of my zany Lynch theories during both projects. To all of them, I will be forever grateful.

Series Foreword

The idea for a series of serious studies of various filmmakers' sonic styles began, as good ideas so often do, with a sidewalk conversation. In this case, the conversation took place during a break between sessions of the Music and the Moving Image conference at New York University in 2011; aside from the fresh air and coffee, its stimulus was the shared observation that since the conference's inception in 2007 there had been a subtle shift in the content of its papers. As one might expect from a conference named the way it is, most of the MaMI papers over the years indeed concentrated on music and its relationship to moving images, usually as demonstrated in singular examples of motion-picture art. But more and more, our sidewalk gang noted, attention was being focused not just on a particular film's music but on all its sonic elements, and not just on the sonic elements of a particular film but on the sonic elements of at least a number of films attributed to the same authorial source.

Thus was born *Music, Sound and Filmmakers: Sonic Style in Cinema* (Routledge, 2012), an edited collection whose dozen chapters deal succinctly yet comprehensively with the "stylish" use of sound by the film producers David O. Selznick and Val Lewton and the film directors Wes Anderson, Ingmar Bergman, the Coen brothers, Peter Greenaway, Krzystof Kiéslowski, Stanley Kubrick, David Lynch, Quentin Tarantino, Andrey Tarkovsky, and Gus Van Sant. In my Preface to that edited collection, I noted that "these twelve scholarly essays on sonic style in cinema represent only a first step on what surely will be a long path." A second step along this path, it surely seems, is Routledge's bold decision to follow up with not merely a sequel to the 2012 collection but with a series of monographs.

Contributors to the *Filmmakers and their Soundtracks* series have been charged, as were the contributors to the 2012 collection, with two questions. Can you imagine a situation in which someone, arriving late to a showing of a film about which he or she has no advance information, might spontaneously say: "Ah, that sounds like a film by so-and-so?" If such a situation can indeed be imagined, then what is it about the film's sonic content that makes it attributable to one particular filmmaker? Like the essays in *Music, Sound and Filmmakers*, the books in the *Filmmakers and their Soundtracks* series seek to answer that more difficult second question by explaining the many and complex reasons why a filmmaker's work, as a whole, has a distinct sonic "trademark."

James Wierzbicki
Series Editor

1 The Sound World of David Lynch

At the opening of 2017's *Twin Peaks: The Return*, The Fireman (Carel Struycken) famously tells Agent Dale Cooper (Kyle Maclachlan) to "listen to the sounds." But to what sounds should he be listening? Those emanating from the Victrola next to Cooper on the end table? Or something else? The Fireman is, albeit indirectly, telling us, the audience, and Cooper, to listen to the sounds around him to better understand the world that we—and he—inhabit. In this way, Lynch immediately makes us aware of the significance of the sound aesthetics.[1]

Chances are that anyone reading this book has at least some familiarity with David Lynch's films, television shows, and internet projects. Eerie, unsettling, and sometimes just plain weird, each film's aesthetic is completed through music and sound design, which Lynch often has a hand in creating, or at the very least for which he makes his intentions known. This close involvement in the creation of his films' music and sound design straddles what Danijela Kulezic-Wilson called "the elaborate interaction between scoring and sound design," the fine line between sensitive and obsessive.[2] Because of Lynch's clear directives about script, sound, music, and image, Allister Mactaggart contends that his films can be considered in the vein of a Wagnerian *Gesamtkunstwerk,* or "total artwork" in which all components are tied to each other.[3] As Tom Kenny has put it, "Nothing about a David Lynch film is 'normal.' Not the script, not the visual stamp, not the editing and certainly not the sound."[4] At the same time, the sound is most distinct: One could likely distinguish a Lynchian film from one that is not by its sounds, which are not only unique but also imaginative.[5] Lynch is more than a director: He is a soundtrack auteur.[6] But this raises a fundamental question: What exactly is the Lynchian sound?

In her essay on the sound of *Lost Highway* (1997), Frances Morgan writes that her first attempt to remember the film took her back to its sonic style before she remembered anything else:

> I did not have to search my mind for *Lost Highway*'s sound, the sound was what I remembered the most: not only was it "the one with Trent Reznor"

DOI: 10.4324/9781003265450-1

> and "the one with Rammstein," it was also, crucially, the one with the video and the drone. It was the one with all the low end: my memory of sitting in the cinema, excited and scared in equal measure by the psychosexual angst and lowering, ominous sonics of *Lost Highway* was filed next to one of emerging from an East London club in the early hours of a morning, ears pummeled by frantic drum and bass, and seeing a meat lorry unload its wares for the next day's market, chilled carcasses steaming in the dawn air. Clangs, drones, beats, flesh, sub-bass, darkness all permeate my memories of that time.[7]

This recollection illustrates the sonic imprint that David Lynch's films leaves on us, an aural fingerprint that is uniquely his.[8] It is not uncommon to hear someone say that something "sounds like a David Lynch movie."

Often, technology plays a crucial role in Lynch's sonic style, one that he has developed since his earliest short films. It is well known that he has an affinity for wind and static, and that he also is fascinated by technological manipulations of music and sound, such as playing a song backwards or at half speed; an example of the latter is Chris Isaak's "In the Heat of the Jungle" in the backyard motel scene of *Wild at Heart*.[9]

Indeed, I have my own experience with Lynch's sonic fingerprint, especially his predilection for industrial sounds. While on a videoconference call one day, I heard a lot of ambient noise that I thought was construction occurring outside my colleague's office on another college campus. I thought it odd that there was a barking dog on the construction site—let alone on campus—and realized only when Henry Spencer (Jack Nance) began to speak that *Eraserhead* (1977) was playing on my computer. The sound was realistic enough that, paired with a lack of dialogue to that point, it seemed plausible that it could be emanating from the other end of my conference call rather than the constructed world of a film.

Defining the Lynchian Sound

"Lynchian" has a relatively simple definition. Zina Giannopoulou has identified a core set of attributes that frequently appear in Lynch's films:

> Non-linear patterns of exposition, intransitive narrative—in which the chain of causation that motivates the action and drives the plot is interrupted or confused through spatial and temporal fragmentation—fluid character identities, a blurry borderland between dreaming and waking life or knowledge and illusion, and loss of memory.[10]

However, determining what it means for a film's sound to be Lynchian is much more difficult. Various scholars have attempted to define this adjective, though these explanations, too, can be pretty vague. Philip Halsall writes that it is "Lynch's keen eye and ear for audio-visual bonds that help to create the 'Lynchian' technique."[11] Randolph Jordan remarks that for a film's aural style to be Lynchian, the sound must "act as the mediator between internal and external worlds."[12] Frances Morgan is slightly more specific, citing what she calls "Lynchian sound realizations" as "the dense, machine presence of *Eraserhead*, the abject, humming mid-range evil of the underrated *Twin Peaks: Fire Walk with Me* (1992), the oppressive domestic drone of *Lost Highway* (1997) and the ominous rumble of much of *Inland Empire* (2006)."[13] Asbjø Skarsvåg Grønstad has recently applied this notion of density, at least in the visuals, to Lynch's work, stating that his work has a certain opacity to it.[14] This density and opacity is clearly found in the director's music and sound design throughout his oeuvre, likely one reason why Steven Willemsen and Miklos Kiss refer to the director's filmic soundscapes as eerie, dark, and dreamy.[15] Zoran Samardzija calls Lynch's signature sound design "ominous."[16]

All of this allows us to call into question what exactly it means for a film's sound to be Lynchian. So far, "dark," "dense," and "opaque" have all been used to describe Lynch's work, all terms that could be applied to the director's original discipline of visual art. Similarly, musician Lykke Li, who has worked with Lynch, describes the Lynchian sound as "a world and a palette."[17] Isabella Van Elferen observes:

> Lynch's complex, destabilizing use of cinematic narration and mediation create ambiguity and uncanniness, his soundtracks intensify that effect to a degree that sometimes verges on the unbearable. As with the visual design of his films, the distinction between and conflation of various levels of auditory perception is crucial. [...] It enables an overlap of diegetic, extradiegetic, and meta-diegetic sound and music.[18]

Van Elferen notes that "in Lynchian sound design dialogue tends to be of sonic rather than narrative value,"[19] and she suggests that different sound levels that accompany the narrative structure function variously. Others, such as Greg Olson, have specifically identified sounds frequently found in Lynch's films. He writes of "the droning sounds, usually of electricity and industry, that he melds with his images; the detailed, close-up fascination with textures."[20] Holly Rogers writes that:

> David Lynch's sonic resonances echo through projects and media. Pulsating room tone, eerie, *acousmêtre*, electronic wash, static drones, thwarted resolutions and remediated retro textures frequently trouble the image, while imploding lip-synchs violently tear sound from sigh and disembodied noises lead attention beyond the edge of the screen. Lynch's soundscapes point beyond themselves.[21]

Similarly, Dennis Lim writes that "to anyone with a passing familiarity with his films—to anyone, or in other words, with a modicum of pop culture literacy—any number of sights and sounds will seem instantly Lynchian," and he cites swelling rumbles on the soundtrack.[22] Keith Phipps reveals that Lynch's sonic style stems from a complex soundscape that makes a film sound Lynchian.[23] Curiously, Michel Chion considers Lynch's sound continuity merely "idiosyncratic."[24]

Others discuss Lynch's sonic ingenuity. Daniel Schweiger notes that "together, Badalamenti and Lynch seemed to have invented their own version of the film soundtrack, a musical purgatory where every kind of style and sound floats about in a beautiful state of dread, all trying to be heard at once—a soundscape that's nothing less than hypnotic."[25] Of his early films with sound designer Alan Splet, Rose Lloyd remarks that "the two of them have created sound-tracks clanking and hissing with noise, as if the world were a factory. The mechanical-biological wheezes, groans, hums, sighs, and wails are perhaps the clearest indication of Lynch's perception of organic reality as machinery breaking down."[26] For Lloyd, then, the mechanical sounds contribute to the Lynchian sound; the organic, natural sounds provide his signature sonic style. Luca Malavasi believes that Lynch's soundscape was already established in his earliest short films, which he describes as featuring background and inhuman sounds.[27] David Foster Wallace remarks that "ominous ambient noises on his soundtracks" are trademark Lynch sounds.[28] Kenneth Kaleta postulates that industrial sounds are the single most identifiable object in Lynch's films.[29] To this, I would add his environmental sounds, which feature prominently in his short films and his first feature-length film, *Eraserhead* (1977), and play an important role in Lynch's filmic sonic style.

But all of these descriptions raise several new questions. What does Halsall mean by "the Lynchian technique"? Does Morgan mean that the "Lynchian sound realizations" are confined to low, industrial sounds only? What makes Lynch's soundscapes both complex and idiosyncratic? Moreover, can we find a central point in all of these descriptions that defines the Lynchian sound? These questions will be answered in detail by the end of this book, but both the Lynchian filmic technique and the Lynchian sound realizations have developed throughout Lynch's career, and they also change depending on whether he uses sound effects, diegetic music, non-diegetic music, or the voice. We can conclude that what makes Lynch's signature sonic style is not only the cohesive sonic style in and across his films but also how he uses them and their narrative purpose. Lynch has often said that sound is "fifty percent of the picture" and "sometimes the sound even overplays the visual," so we must understand his preferences for the use of sound in his films and how their use becomes so sonically distinct.[30]

One would think that a clear definition of the Lynchian sound might come from a close collaborator with the director. In a phone interview with Dean

Hurley, sound designer for *Inland Empire*, *The Return*, and *What Did Jack Do*?, I asked him to define the director's sonic style. He replied:

> It's a complex tapestry of different influences. I would kind of liken it to the ingredients for a cake. All of his specific different ingredients come together. But without the egg, it's not going to levitate like a cake; if you take one of the ingredients out, it just doesn't work. And so, it's several strands of things that make up several key ingredients that make up his sort of sensibility, and they're not always present in equal amounts. But if I had a gun to my head and I had to come up with an answer, I would just start listing the things. He, more than any other director, has an ear toward the importance of what lower frequencies can do in terms of the sound design. His stuff isn't one shade. A lot of people will use the word dark, but it's not. It's never simply dark; it's always contrasted with an incredible contrasting beauty or lightness about it. There's an extremity to his own usages of lower frequency and sometimes Angelo's beautiful score. It's really hard to pinpoint. I think I'm going to fail you on this, because I can't really give it give a concise-ish statement or example. I mean, it's very difficult.
>
> I think the fool's journey would be to try to say "this is the David Lynch sound." A few years ago, there was like this tendency to mash up a YouTube trailer like *A Very Goofy Movie,* the Disney animated film in the style of a David Lynch trailer, or what's the other one I saw? *Last Dance* or *Footloose* or something like that as a trailer in the David Lynch style. It was like a goofy experiment that people were doing saying, "Okay, let's just combine these two flavors and you get a lot of the ingredients that have sort of been done before." So, you get sort of this one dimensionality to somebody putting in a low drone or maybe somebody screaming but it's slowed down and exaggerated and reality becomes warped at a certain point. But he doesn't necessarily think like these are paint-by-numbers sort of things that he ends up employing again and again. I think there's motifs that he reaches for, but he'll also pull something new out of thin air that becomes another shade to his formula. I think you could distill all the different film examples over time. There's this component [and] there's this component. But in reality, I think he's looking at the medium like he's finding backdoor ways to amplify or push things to the outer extremity. I would always become amazed at his use of language to communicate his ideas before something exists to his practitioners, whether it be the cinematographer or Angelo or a vocalist or an actor. And he would always find just an odd succinct image word choice or something that would crystallize the idea. If the scale is 1 to 10, he would paint something to get an 11, 12, or 13 out of somebody. I could say that the only through-line is he wants the edge, the extreme extremity. The words beautiful [and] dark

> have always been tossed around when talking about his work, but his seeds are darker than most or the upper echelon is more beautiful than some of the other things—it's always a wide extreme. And it's a kind of a melt your ears extreme that he's after.[31]

This begs the question: If a close collaborator cannot define the Lynchian sound, then why should the rest of us even try? The answer lies in the big picture.

To define what makes up Lynch's signature sound, we must consider his typical filmic sounds dating from his earliest works. For one, the industrial sound has formed the cornerstone of an aural style that has become known as Lynchian. But Lynch himself dislikes the term, and avoids defining it; when Dennis Lim asked Lynch to define it, Lynch famously changed the subject.[32] But Lynch is less reluctant to talk about the sound of his work. When specifically asked about his favorite sounds, he remarked:

> There's not one particular kind of sound that I like but if I had to pick a category it would be factory sounds. I like the power of them and it makes a picture in my mind … . I like the idea of factories and factory life probably because I don't know that much about them. I can just imagine a world and it leads to a bigger place where many strange and beautiful things can happen.[33]

Although Lynch favors industrial sounds, his films are not limited to them. He also uses sounds that imitate the environment where they are found. My use of the word "imitate" is deliberate here; often Lynch does not use sounds as they are found in nature but instead uses other sources to create similar sounds. Lynch's music and sound design are so intertwined that it is almost impossible to separate them.

One such sound for which Lynch is known is electricity. Dean Hurley mentioned that Lynch tends to use very specific sounds, such as the sounds of electricity, in multiple works. He stated:

> It's not just that he's interested in it from a sonic perspective, it's that he's interested in a massive concept, and like a magical notion, so it's like he becomes entranced with the kind of proverbial, noticing things that are commonplace like the powerlines everywhere. He's becoming enchanted by this notion of us as a civilization [who] have become reliant upon this and we're literally stringing wires between the entire population over continents and it connects everyone. It's an enchanting concept. And so, I think when he gets bitten by a sort of a concept like that, it's like a holistic concept that ends up rippling out into everything. And sonically, it's like let's explore that visually. It's like a multi-dimensional idea because he talks about the idea a lot, but sometimes these ideas have a DNA structure

> that you can keep looking at through a microscope and get deeper, deeper layers, and there's harmonic overtones to the idea, like music. You can have a pure sine wave, but the complexity of the piano note, it's 440. But it's not a 440 sine wave, there's more harmonic multiples happening that make a complexity and provide the timbre of that sound. So, when you look at that one sound, it's comprised of many harmonic frequencies. And I think that's how an idea like electricity operates. For him, it sort of harmonically resonates through many different areas and then, as a result, the fabric of the work sort of congeals in this way, because they're working conceptually and also pragmatically and there's all these things happening together. And it's got a deeper resonance.[34]

Lynch's approach to sound is very intuitive from the perspective of someone who works with him but very deliberate from the perspective of those who do not work with him. Therefore, there are a plethora of meanings, but no single meaning, of the Lynchian sound.

But it is not only the "what" of Lynch's films but also the "how" that is important. Of any director, Lynch plays the greatest role in his films' sound design, many times assuming the role of the sound designer himself or working alongside a sound designer or composer. Danijela Kulezic-Wilson has observed that "sound is usually a reliable indicator of significant changes in perception or the mental space of characters. … Sound has always been deeply embedded in the Lynchian universe, seeping through the porous borders of its morphing subplots in order to either connect bizarre episodes and temporal digressions or to mark shifts between them."[35]

Writing on *The Return,* but applicable to all of Lynch's works, Steven Wilson notes that "The sound world … is rich in meaning, with a spectrum extending from abstraction to explicit referentiality."[36] Aside from their unique sound designs, Lynch's films are known for their use of diegetic and non-diegetic popular songs, sometimes from the most unlikely and diverse artists. The types of musicians he features in his films contribute to his signature sound.[37] But this distinctive sound extends beyond his use of popular songs in his films; it is *what* popular songs he uses and *how* he chooses to use them that leave his distinctive sonic imprint. Lynch is systematic about what songs he chooses to use in his films and, although sometimes his use of diegetic music comes from one of his "happy accidents," such as Rebekah Del Rio's performance of "Llorando" in *Mulholland Drive* (2001), he chooses certain songs for their overarching aesthetic value rather than their underlying meaning.[38]

I contend that, if we consider the music—both diegetic and non-diegetic—sound effects, sound design, and use of the voice, we can divide what we know as the Lynchian sonic style into three phases, which, unsurprisingly, have evolved along with Lynch's filmic style: the short films for which he created the music and sound design alone, his work with sound designers

Alan Splet and Randy Thom, and his later collaborations with composers John Morris and Angelo Badalamenti and sound designer Dean Hurley. We can further divide each of these phases by how Lynch uses sound: ambient sounds, diegetic music, non-diegetic music, and the voice, and how he plays with audience expectations about what is diegetic and what is not. These different functions and phases form uniquely and distinctly Lynchian sound profiles. The first phase (1966–77) includes his early short films and *Eraserhead.* The second phase (1980–84) consists of *The Elephant Man* through *Dune*, with his collaborations with John Morris and Alan Splet. The third phase (1986–2020) includes his collaborations with Angelo Badalamenti, Randy Thom, John Ross, and Dean Hurley. Each chapter in this book covers one or more of the phases and sound techniques, but there are frequent overlaps between sonic elements. For example, we cannot discuss sound effects, dubbing, or voice without discussing volume, and we cannot discuss Americana music without discussing both diegetic and non-diegetic music.

We can identify the various Lynchian sounds because of his generally long-term collaborations with specific composers and sound designers. Despite this, even when Lynch begins to work with another collaborator, he knows what he wants and continues his work along the same stylistic lines, using the same techniques. For example, when working with Splet on *Eraserhead*, Lynch made the sounds by recording through bottles and tubes. In *Lost Highway*, he did the same thing when working alone and with post-production sound editor John Ross.[39]

Lynch's Early Short Films: Beginnings of a Sound Profile

To understand how Lynch came to be known for his films' sonic profile, we must examine the role of music and sound in his earliest films. As Lynch once articulated: "Sound is almost like a drug. It's so pure that when it goes in your ears, it instantly does something to you. And you can tell if that's working for you."[40] Once he found a sound that worked for him, Lynch continued to produce that kind of sound with few alterations. Lim refers to these early films as "transitional," but I believe that they should be more accurately called "formational."[41]

Lynch's sonic style derived from his earliest films, namely those short films that he made either while a student at the American Film Institute (AFI) or shortly thereafter: *Six Men Getting Sick* (1966), *Absurd Encounter with Fear* (1967), *Fictitious Anacin Commercial* (1968), *The Alphabet* (1968), *The Grandmother* (1970), and *The Amputee* (1974). His first feature-length film, the film that employs his first attempt to create a signature sound profile that he started to develop in these early films, is *Eraserhead* (1977). Ambient industrial sounds, which influenced Lynch when he lived in Philadelphia where he made these early films, pervaded his early short films and *Eraserhead.*[42] Lynch's predilection for setting his films in small insular locations, whether

Philadelphia in *Eraserhead* or a living room in *The Amputee*, establishes his sonic profile.[43]

While Lynch was an art student in Philadelphia, a painting once mesmerized him, and he wondered as he stared at it what would happen if it moved.[44] This led to the creation of his earliest film, a short called *Six Men Getting Sick* (sometimes referred to as *Six Figures Getting Sick,* sometimes with the subtitle "Six Times"). The four-minute film uses animation of a Lynch drawing of six men vomiting and bleeding into containers as their faces become disfigured.

Six Men Getting Sick includes a short yet prolonged sound throughout its duration. The images form a single continually looped 41-second pattern that plays over the siren. This technique allowed him to use a single effect with minimal cost but also made it easy for him to use his preferred sounds.[45] Alan Splet liked working with industrial sounds because they created many possibilities, which is one of the reasons why, although industrial sounds can be found throughout Lynch's oeuvre, no two sound effects are alike.[46] The film's use of sound does, however, differ slightly from Lynch's later films in that where an extended sound occurs, as is the case here, it will often abruptly cease mid-shot.[47] These sound cuts are at their most obvious and frequently used in *Eraserhead,* creating the continuity through interruption for which Lynch is known.[48] Other than the siren and industrial sounds, there is no music or sound in *Six Men Getting Sick*. Olson calls the sound design of this film "an assaultive experience for spectators."[49] We can extend this description of the sound design to all of Lynch's films, which all feature harsh and loud sounds that can be heard daily on city streets. This attempt to ground a film in one aural aesthetic gave rise to his easily identifiable sonic style in his later films.

Approximately two years after *Six Men Getting Sick*, Lynch made another short film, *The Alphabet*, which took his use of sound one step further. Lynch was fascinated with the sound of wind and he incorporated it into this film. He recounted that hearing the wind when he first thought about filmmaking played an important role in his conception of sound design; hearing the wind at the same time that he saw an object move made him realize the importance of sound in a moving image, and he understood that both must move seamlessly together.

The sounds for *The Alphabet* resulted from one of Lynch's happy accidents. He went to an industrial film lab in Philadelphia, Calvin de Frenes, to rent a Uher tape recorder. Upon beginning his recording session, he realized that the tape recorder was broken and distorting all of his sounds which, it turned out, he loved. He then took these sounds back into Calvin de Frenes and used their four-track mixing console to create the film's sounds—but not before telling them about the broken tape recorder, which they let him keep.[50]

The Alphabet consists of drawings interspersed with short live-action segments. These drawings are first accompanied by children chanting the letters A-B-C, but this soon morphs into Lynch's friend, Robert Chadwick, singing an operatic-like vocalise. Later there is a recitation of the entire alphabet combined with the sounds of a crying baby (Lynch's infant daughter, Jennifer) and the cooing mother.[51] Chadwick's singing and the singing of the alphabet song are the only music in the film; Lynch's sounds here are organic for the first time. There are other sounds in the film, though, such as that of the siren (which again was the only sound in his first short film, *Six Men Getting Sick*), humming that sounds like a vibration or buzzing, and whistling. This whistling moves into the sound of the wind as the humming is electronically manipulated; the siren sound fluctuates as if manipulated by an oscillator. Chris Rodley reads this film as the overcoming of non-verbality and, as some have noted, Lynch wrote this film when he was in his "pre-verbal" stage, when he was known to communicate via gesture rather than words.[52]

While his first films began to establish his filmic sonic profile, Lynch has referred to *The Amputee* throughout his career as one of his most significant, especially concerning its sound. This was also his first completely live-action film rather than a mix of live action with animation, as in *The Alphabet* or *The Grandmother*. He produced it four years after *The Grandmother*, and for this he would return to the format of the short four-minute film. *The Amputee* was his first film to use both the Foley process and recorded voice-over dialogue because the film stock was incapable of handling synchronized sound.[53] Lynch recorded the sound effects and added them through the post-production Foley process.[54] Most of the film's sound comes from a voiceover of the on-screen actress (Catherine Coulson), who edits a letter she is writing. We also hear many ambient sounds in the room such as the slamming of doors, the running and splashing of water, and sounds the nurse makes (David Lynch) as he clips her bandages when cleaning her wounds. Here, Lynch progressively moves toward the use of the ambient sounds that are present in the character's environment rather than musical underscoring, and this creates a sense of realism.

Roots of Features in Sound: *The Grandmother*

Lynch's early films have mostly been around four minutes in length, but *The Grandmother* is the longest film of his early period that was not a feature, lasting over a half hour and allowing for a greater sonic development than in any of his earlier works. We can see this film as the germination of his sonic style that we find throughout the remainder of his career. *The Grandmother* was the film that established Lynch's future sound profile in its most mature form.[55] As we have seen, aside from industrial sounds, Lynch prefers organic sounds, and this is clearest in *The Grandmother*; many of the organic sound effects that we hear in *Eraserhead* and other later films first appear here.[56] Both animation and stop motion camera work are found in *The Grandmother*, giving it a visual profile distinct from those of his earlier films. However, the sonic profile is an outgrowth of these early films. We can hear the maturation of Lynch's sonic style because of the film's length. Because it is longer than all his films thus far, *The Grandmother* provides a greater opportunity for narrative development through sound.

The film features a boy named Mark (Richard White) who lives with a set of verbally and physically abusive parents (Virginia Maitland and Robert Chadwick) and creates for himself a kind grandmother (Dorothy McGinnis) by planting seeds. There is a plethora of organic sounds from the barking of dogs, which represent Mark's parents' verbal abuse, to the flowing of urine as he wets his bed. Some of these sounds are amplified so that they do not go unnoticed as typically some of these sounds might. We can see the beginnings of this in *The Amputee* with the sound of dripping water and the cutting of bandages. Some of the sounds in *The Grandmother* simply came from existing sound effects recordings.[57]

The sound generation for *The Grandmother* is Lynch's first step in creating a distinct sonic profile, one that includes the continuous blurring of sound, image, and narrative.[58] In this film:

> Lynch uses sound as a fourth wall, as it were, a spatial agent in its own right. Lynch's use of noises creates not only a musical score, but also forms a special audio narrative for the viewer, offering unique view-points. There are background noises, "room-tones," silence and dialogue. They interlock with the visual story of Lynch's films in a Moebius string sense, or rather, as "red herrings" in a propaganda sense, distracting the viewer's attention, and often creating further mystery.[59]

The film features some of Lynch's future techniques, such as abrupt sound cuts mid-shot, sound simultaneity, and the use of extended sound effects and room tone.[60] Without sound, Lynch's films might be hard-pressed to interact with the viewers in the way they do. Lynch himself affirms this simultaneity: "By putting different sounds over the same image, you can create such different types of feelings."[61] This type of sound layering became a hallmark of Lynch's films throughout his career.

For Lynch, necessity was the mother of invention when it came to creating sound. While making *The Grandmother*, he went to the Calvin de Frenes Studio with the intention to work with his usual sound designer, Bob Collum, to obtain sound effects. However, Collum was too busy to work with Lynch at the time so he paired him with another sound designer, Alan Splet, creating a working relationship that would last for several decades. Upon the pair going through the available sound effects in the library, Lynch felt that none would work for the film, so he and Splet made them from scratch.[62] It took Lynch and Splet 12 hours per day for 63 days to create and record the necessary sound effects.[63] His sister Margaret Lynch and Bob Chadwick also helped Lynch with the sound design.[64] In an interview, Splet explained his and Lynch's process for creating the film's sound design:

> Some of the effects we got off records, but most of it we made ourselves. All we had was a couple of 16mm dubbers and a little tiny board. And we were making effects out of (the sound of) pencil sharpeners and plungers and junk in the machine shop and whatever we could get out hands on. We wanted to reverb a whistle. David actually made the whistle, and we didn't have any reverb device. So we took a piece of aluminum heat ducting, which we found in the shop, and put a speaker on one end and a microphone on the other, blew the whistle and we got a little reverb. Not really much, so we put it through again, maybe 20 times, and kept re-recording it through this thing to get enough reverb on it because we didn't have a proper reverb device. That's all we knew so that's how we did it.[65]

This process of creating a complete sound effects library for a film from nothing was something that Lynch did for every film after *The Grandmother* and still continues to do. Because of the film's unique industrial sound, some have described its score as an example of *musique concrète*.[66]

The Grandmother's sounds are very mechanical, including rotating and grinding noises. In several places there is a descending, oscillating perfect fourth ostinato combined with a grinding sound under it. There are also the sounds of wind, which Lynch continually uses in his later films, and there are the amplified sounds of everyday actions. For instance, the shaking as Mark throws the seeds from the bag is dubbed loudly, and the crinkling sound as Mark throws the buckets of dirt on the bed is also amplified. Nighttime sounds from crickets occur as Mark spreads the dirt to plant the rock on the bed, concluding with the sound of a bomb explosion and its sizzle as he waters the rock. There is also a squealing sound like that of the *Eraserhead* baby as the grandmother grows. When Mark waters the grandmother's pod again later, it sounds like a thunderstorm with heavy rain. Lynch also uses a moaning sound with heavy reverberation during the dinner scene.

We hear other amplified sounds in the film, especially toward the end. There is a sustained whistle like that of a tea kettle as the grandmother dies in bed; the sound varies depending on the distance Mark is from her, but it is continuous. We hear organ chords underneath as Mark tries to get help from his parents. His mother laughs at him but we can only hear the whistle and organ chord. The drone returns when Mark is in the cemetery and we see the grandmother sitting in a chair. She throws her head back, accompanied by a piercing organ note, as she and Mark silently scream. The film ends with Mark in bed, with the sound of footsteps turning into scratching and cracking turning into a drone.

Without using words, Lynch represents his characters' attributes. Dissonant sound effects that aurally demonstrate their degenerate and abusive nature accompany his parents. The parents are also given a speech impediment when they try to say Mark's name; it often sounds like "Mike." The grandmother, on the other hand, makes multiple sounds, such as roaring, squeaking, and bleeding as she is born (akin to the sound of the chicken in the dinner scene in *Eraserhead*), and there are bird sounds throughout the film, some of which the grandmother makes, as I will discuss below. These are early plays on the voice that Lynch's later films feature.

The Grandmother is Lynch's first film to use animal sounds rather than dialogue to tell the story. Andrea Halskov hypothesizes that:

> the animalistic sounds illustrate the primal and uncontrollable actions of the two parents—the father seemingly barking at his son while correcting him, and the mother sounding like a whimpering dog while caressing and pulling at her son in a strangely sexual fashion. The libidinal and destructive urges, which we usually keep down or silence, are heard on the soundtrack, and the use of extreme close-ups and unnaturalistic colors also serve to de-humanize the parents or to illustrate their animalistic side.[67]

Animal sounds prove important in Lynch's films and appear in almost all of them, even as recently as *The Return.* Mark's parents whimper and bark like dogs, and make monkey sounds, likely to draw attention to their animalistic nature.[68] One of the more interesting sounds in *The Grandmother* is the use of a bird's chirping. This chirping is at its most conspicuous when the grandmother dies, which Kaleta likens to her "choking in her own chirping sounds, fluttering madly around the room like a captured bird smashing itself against the confines of its cage."[69]

Lynch also uses the organ in this film, and the organ appears in several other later films including *Eraserhead.* We hear minor-key plagal cadences played on the organ that announce the grandmother's birth. Later, the organ returns, but with the theme from a song by the band Tractor. There is also an organ drone through most of the film. Like the organ, the organic sounds in the film indicate a time and place, and these different techniques find their way into Lynch's ambitious film, *Eraserhead.*

Lynch's First Feature Film: *Eraserhead*

Aside from its visual uncanniness, *Eraserhead*'s aural profile has helped to establish for Lynch the mature sonic profile that continues in his later works. One of the hallmarks of Lynch's filmic sound profile, from *Eraserhead* onward, is that sound creates a distorted sense of reality in how it plays with the diegesis, while at the same time remaining faithful to the kinds of sounds one might hear in reality.[70] We cannot always tell if what we hear is emanating from an off-screen source as part of the diegesis or if it is non-diegetic, and this sonic ambiguity often occurs in Lynch's later feature films and television shows.

Part of what makes *Eraserhead* so sonically interesting is the fact that it was made over a period of many years as opposed to several months, as was the case with Lynch's other early films. Therefore, we can get a sense of how Lynch's concept of sound design changed over the course of several years; this provides insight into what to expect about Lynch's thoughts on sound design's role in film throughout his career. One of the most characteristic sound elements in *Eraserhead* is sound layering, often featuring industrial and organic sounds. The sound layering provides a sense of being between two worlds, something that Lynch's films constantly examine. Many of the film's sounds are also anempathetic, further displacing the viewer.[71]

As with many of Lynch's early films, the sound design in *Eraserhead* is necessarily harsh. Just as Olson has described the sound of *Six Men Getting Sick* as assaultive, likewise K. George Godwin has described *Eraserhead* as "an auditory and visual assault which isolates each viewer."[72] As stated above, the industrial sounds of his Philadelphia neighborhood influenced Lynch when making *Eraserhead*, but there was another impetus behind it: what he calls "room tone." He recalls:

> I'm real fascinated by presences—what you call "room tone." It's the sound that you hear when there's silence, in between words or sentences. It's a tricky thing, because in this seemingly kind of quiet sound, some feelings can be brought in, and a certain kind of picture of a bigger world can be made. And all those things are important to make that world.[73]

These presences, or room tones, would quickly find a place in all of the director's films, regardless of whether the viewer notices them. Chapter 2 discusses room tone in Lynch's films more broadly.

Sometimes Lynch uses sound effects not to tell a story but simply because he likes the aesthetics they create; a good example of this is the sound of the power station in *Eraserhead*. *Eraserhead* is Lynch's first film to use electricity sounds, which appear in later films such as *Inland Empire* and *Fire Walk With Me*.[74] We can also infer that the use of sound for aesthetic purposes applies also to the sounds of the wind.[75] However, despite Lynch's enjoyment of industrial sounds, any sounds used in the film had to be deliberate. For this reason, they shot *Eraserhead* at night to avoid ambient noise.[76] The sound worlds in Lynch's early films typically function as visual support, especially in *Eraserhead*, so that the viewer must construct meaning similar to how a listener would do the same while listening to a golden-age radio drama.[77] Volume also plays a crucial role here. As we see the character of Henry walk home, Lynch varies the volume of the soundtrack to create a sense of mood and atmosphere.[78]

But Lynch does not use the sound sources unaltered, and this sound manipulation and distortion occurs in his other films. He and Alan Splet electronically manipulated sounds so that they would take on a new, often ethereal, quality, but they did not synthesize any sounds.[79] The pair distorted not only the industrial sounds but also vocal sounds. Lynch recounted that they made these changes "with a graphic equalizer, reverb, a Little Dipper filter set for peaking certain frequencies and dipping out things or reversing things or cutting things together."[80] They altered the pitches, but not the playback speed. Lynch specifically notes that in doing so, the sounds in the film function as characters.[81]

The pair used a process of elimination to make the sounds for *Eraserhead.* Lynch remembered that he and Splet would take the electronic sound material that they generated and "start off with a regular sound and altering it in lots of different ways and trying different things, until we got something that was right for one little thing."[82] Lynch continues to create sounds by testing different combinations and to do this, his intuition guides him. As Hurley says:

> I think a lot of film directors are one-dimensionally concerned about the actor's performance; so many other things are whizzing by their awareness. But with David, the awareness is so piqued and so high. I think that the misconception is that a director thinks about all this stuff beforehand. It's like he or she has the whole movie in their head and they've religiously done storyboards or this or that, and they can see the whole thing, but I think the scene for David is completely abstract. It's not just seeing—it's feeling, the resultant sort of vibration of the sea. So, whenever something is slightly off, out of place, or lacking, it's like a simple gesture to fill that in, is where the strong suit is.[83]

Yet, despite the sounds' organic nature, how Lynch uses them often "denaturalizes the audiovisual scene."[84]

For many people, *Eraserhead* was the first of Lynch's films they encountered, and its sound was nothing short of unsettling. After the film's release, some people said that its sounds had some unusual effects on them. Slavoj Žižek writes that after *Eraserhead*'s premiere, "a strange rumor began to circulate to account for its traumatic impact: At the time, it was rumored that an ultra-low frequency drone in the film's soundtrack affected the viewer's subconscious mind. People said that although inaudible, this noise caused a feeling of unease, even nausea."[85] Whether or not this story is true, it remains a testament to Lynch's unconventional filmic sound world.

Lynch constantly strove to manipulate the audience's perspective. As Greg Hainge points out:

> The almost constant background noise becomes the aural accompaniment not only of the world in which the protagonist Henry lives, but that of the viewer, too. The noise permeating *Eraserhead* is an industrial drone which

> suggests that the viewer is inhabiting a mechanical world, a world which is a production-line for sound.[86]

All *Eraserhead*'s sounds were, as Lynch put it, organic, but they never derived from the source from which they were supposed to come. For instance, he did not use sounds from a baby in the film, and he often refused to say what he did use to make this or the other organic sounds.[87] Yet when he did specify the origins of a sound, he was oddly specific, such as this example from *Eraserhead* when Henry is making love to his neighbor across the hall:[88]

> Very, very little of the sound was real at all. We concocted and made every single sound. One sound we made, for the love scene, was, we took a bathtub, and floated a Sparklettes bottle in the bathtub; we had a microphone down inside the Sparklettes bottle. Then we had a garden hose inside the Sparklettes bottle, and at the other end of the hose, someone blew air into the bottle while, I don't know, Alan was probably doing it, but I was moving the bottle around in the tub like this, and it would make like a little ringing, very subtle, a dreamy ringing, and this air moving in there had a tone to it, and it would change as it moved around.[89]

Lynch reveals the sound effects' unconventional function in the film, stating that "at times the sound/noise changes with each shot in the same scene. It is used as atmosphere, almost as a character, and is a memorable part of the film."[90] Aside from the use of hoses and bottles, deadened sound—made by the use of sound-deadening blankets that Splet manufactured and then nailed to the studio walls during recording—and white noise pervaded the *Eraserhead* soundtrack, giving it a very distinct sound from other films in theaters at the time (and even since).[91] Notably, the soundtrack sounds mechanical.[92] Todd McGowan suggests that the film's vitality derives from the sound of machines.[93]

Eraserhead, in effect, lacked a musical score in the traditional sense, with the exception of the infrequent use of Fats Waller's organ music that emanates from the Victrola in Henry's room.[94] Rather, the score consisted of a compilation of carefully crafted, overlapped, and merged sound effects throughout the film, created because Lynch felt that music is brittle but sound effects are liquid.[95] In the case of a film such as *Eraserhead* where the sound effects blur into the music, Lynch describes this sonic blurring as "a stretchy in-between thing."[96] This sound is what Godwin describes as "a remarkably intricate, expressionistic sound track" that "take[s] the viewer on detours which seem to lead back to our starting point—but not quite."[97] There were other sonic conventions established in the film that would become an important part of Lynch's later films, such as the use of sound devices like the turntable or Victrola.[98]

Conclusion

The presence and absence of sound in Lynch's films help to establish a Lynchian sonic style.[99] Although Lynch's sonic style has evolved over time, it has its roots in his earliest works and during his time as a visual artist. We can understand Lynch's early sonic style as a product of his interest in industrial and organic sounds and the construction of objects from unusual items. Indeed, many of these sound-making techniques and sonic profiles occur in his later feature films.

Given Lynch's use of sound, we can determine what it means for the early films to have "a Lynchian sound." In these films, there is a focus on sound mechanization and the use of natural and organic sounds. Rather than music as underscore, there is an emphasis on ambient and mechanical sounds. Further, these ambient sounds are employed, amplified, and distorted such that sometimes the listener can misconstrue them as underscoring, often unaware that they are not until a certain point in the narrative is reached. We can also conclude that the use of ambient sound in Lynch's early films creates a narrative drive not found in the films of other directors.[100] Specifically, Lynch thrives on sounds, such as those of wind and electricity, and these become sonic staples in his later films.

Lynch's use of material for his organic sounds is not only carefully manipulated but also derived from sources other than what they seem to be. The sound of a baby crying is rarely the actual sound of a baby crying; it might be a cat meowing with the sound drawn through filters and sped up or slowed down (or both). Lynch adds reverberation and echo effects to further alter some of these sounds. In this way, he removes reality from the film, allowing the sound to contribute to a film's uncanniness. He also layers and mixes sounds so that they create a sense of disorientation—temporal or otherwise. As Laura Dern has remarked, Lynch "definitely wants to create a world where you never know where you are."[101]

The next chapter considers Lynch's sonic style through an examination of his sound design, mainly focusing on the creation, use, role of, and distinction between sound and ambient noise, and how these have evolved over time while still adhering to Lynch's typical sonic style. The discussion will draw on films discussed in this chapter to show how Lynch's sound aesthetics in his later films extended from his early career; it will consider how Lynch blended music and sound in his feature films, and how he used ambient sound to create a world or a sense of being between two (or more) worlds.

Notes

1 Jessica Getman, "Playing with Sound: Fan Engagement with the Soundtrack of *Twin Peaks: The Return* (2017)," in *The Music of Twin*

Peaks: Listen to the Sounds, eds. Reba Wissner and Katherine Reed (Abingdon and New York: Routledge, 2021), 34.

2 Danijela Kulezic-Wilson, *Sound Design Is the New Score: Theory, Aesthetics, and Erotics of the Integrated Soundtrack* (Oxford and New York: Oxford University Press, 2020), 64; Clare Nina Norelli, "Suburban Dread: The Music of Angelo Badalamenti in the Films of David Lynch," in *Sound Scripts: Proceedings of the 2007 Totally Huge New Music Festival*, Vol. 2, eds. Cat Hope and Jonathan W. Marshall (New South Wales: Australian Music Centre, 2009), 38.

3 Allister Mactaggart, "'I Am Dead, Yet I Live': Revealing the Enigma of Art in *Twin Peaks: The Return*," *NANO: New American Notes Online* 15 (2020), https://nanocrit.com/issues/issue15/I-am-dead-yet-I-live-Revealing-the-Enigma-of-Art-in-Twin-Peaks-The-Return.

4 Tom Kenny, *Sound for Picture: Film Sound Through the 1990s* (Vallejo, CA: Mix Books, 2000), 128.

5 John Alexander, *The Films of David Lynch* (Edinburgh: Charles Letts and Co., 1993), 21.

6 Annette Davison, "Demystified, Remystified, and Seduced by Sirens: Listening to David Lynch's Films," in *Essays on Sound and Vision*, eds. John Richardson and Stan Hawkins (Yliopistopaino: Helsinki University Press, 2007), 129.

7 Frances Morgan, "Darkness Audible: Sub-Bass, Tape Decay and Lynchian Noise," in *The End: An Electric Sheep Anthology*, ed. Virginia Selavy (London: Strange Attractor Press, 2011), 192.

8 Philip Halsall, *The Films of David Lynch: 50 Percent Sound* (London: British Film Resource, 2002), accessed October 2, 2018, http://www.britishfilm.org.uk/lynch/Sintro.html.

9 Emma Griffiths, "Q&A with David Lynch's Music Collaborator Dean Hurley – Part 1: Working On and 'Protecting The Experience' of *Twin Peaks: The Return*," *Synchtank*, July 21, 2017, accessed July 30, 2018, https://www.synchtank.com/blog/qa-with-david-lynchs-music-collaborator-dean-hurley-part-1-working-on-and-protecting-the-experience-of-twin-peaks-the-return/.

10 Zina Giannopoulou, "Introduction," in *Mulholland Drive*, ed. Zina Giannopolou (London and New York: Routledge, 2013), 2.

11 Halsall, *The Films of David Lynch*.

12 Randolph Jordan, "Starting from Scratch: Turntables, Auditory Representation, and the Structure of the Known Universe in the Films of David Lynch" (MA Thesis, Concordia University, Canada, 2003), 124.

13 Morgan, "Darkness Audible: Sub-Bass, Tape Decay and Lynchian Noise," 188.

14 Asbjø Skarsvåg Grønstad, *Rethinking Art and Visual Culture: The Poetics of Opacity* (Springer International Publishing AG, 2020), 117.

15 Steven Willemsen and Miklos Kiss, "Last Year at Mulholland Drive: Ambiguous Framings and Framing Ambiguities," *Acta Universitatis Sapentiae, Film and Media Studies* 16 (2019): 138, 143.

16 Zoran Samardzija, "DavidLynch.com: Auteurship in the Age of the Internet and Digital Cinema," *Scope* 16 (2012), accessed February 12, 2019, https://www.nottingham.ac.uk/scope/documents/2010/february-2010/samardzija.pdf.

17 Lior Phillips, "Lykke Li and Dean Hurley Explain What 'Lynchian' Means: David Lynch's Past Collaborators Pull Aside The Red Velvet Curtains,"

Consequence of Sound, September 2, 2017, accessed October 3, 2018, https://consequenceofsound.net/2017/09/lykke-li-and-dean-hurley-explain-what-lynchian-means/.

18 Isabella Van Elferen, "Dream Timbre: Notes on Lynchian Sound Design," in *Music, Sound, and Filmmakers: Sonic Style in Cinema*, ed. James Wierzbicki (New York and Abingdon: Routledge, 2012), 179.

19 Van Elferen, "Dream Timbre," 179–80.

20 Greg Olson, *David Lynch: Beautiful Dark* (Lanham, MD and Toronto: Scarecrow Press, 2008), 3.

21 Holly Rogers, "The Audiovisual Eerie: Transmediating Thresholds in the Work of David Lynch," in *Transmedia Directors: Artistry, Industry and the New Audiovisual Aesthetics*, eds. Carol Vernallis, Holly Rogers, and Lisa Perrott (New York: Bloomsbury, 2019), 241.

22 Dennis Lim, *David Lynch: The Man from Another Place* (New York: Amazon Publishing, 2015), 6.

23 Keith Phipps, "Industrial Soundscapes: *Eraserhead/Lost Highway/Inland Empire*," in *Beyond the Beyond: Music from the Films of David Lynch*, eds. J. C. Gabel and Jessica Hundley (Los Angeles: Hat and Beard Press, 2016), 91.

24 Michel Chion, *David Lynch*, trans. Robert Julian (London: British Film Institute, 1995), 44.

25 Daniel Schweiger, "The Madman and His Muse," *Film Score Monthly* (September 2001): 24.

26 Rose Lloyd, "Tumoresque: The Films of David Lynch," *Atlantic*, October 1984, 108.

27 Luca Malavasi, *Mulholland Drive* (Turin: Lindau, 2008), 12.

28 David Foster Wallace, "David Lynch Keeps His Head," in *A Supposedly Fun Thing I'll Never Do Again: Essays and Arguments* (New York: Little, Brown, and Co., 1997), 150–1.

29 Kenneth C. Kaleta, *David Lynch* (New York: Twayne Publishers, 1992), 64.

30 David Hughes, *The Complete Lynch* (London: Virgin Publishing, 2001), 23; "The Monster Meets…Filmmaker David Lynch," *The Home Theater Buyers Guide* (Fall 1998), accessed March 1, 2019, http://www.lynchnet.com/monster.html.

31 Phone interview with Dean Hurley, May 21, 2021.

32 Lim, *David Lynch*, 5.

33 Alexander, *The Films of David Lynch*, 45.

34 Phone interview with Dean Hurley, May 21, 2021.

35 Danijela Kulezic-Wilson, *The Musicality of Narrative Film* (Houndsmills and Basingstoke: Palgrave Macmillan, 2015), 109.

36 Steven Wilson, "David Lynch's Metaphysical Sound Design: The Acousmatic Personification of Judy," in *The Music of Twin Peaks: Listen to the Sounds*, ed. Reba Wissner and Katherine Reed (Abingdon and New York: Routledge, 2021), 153.

37 Lim, *David Lynch*, 72.

38 Griffiths, "Q&A with David Lynch's Music Collaborator Dean Hurley."

39 Kenny, *Sound for Picture*, 132.

40 Andy Klein, "Director's Notes," *The Hollywood Reporter*, Film & TV Music Special Issue, 1990, accessed December 12, 2018, http://www.thecityofabsurdity.com/intmusic.html.

41 Lim, *David Lynch*, 39.

42 Liz Greene, "Bringing Vinyl into The Digital Domain: Aesthetics in David Lynch's *Inland Empire* (2006)," *The New Soundtrack* 2, no. 2 (2012): 103.

43 Richard Martin, "Neighborhoods or Nothing? Social Relations in David Lynch's *Blue Velvet*," *European Journal of American Culture* 32, no. 3 (2013): 238–9.

44 David Lynch, *The Art Life*, DVD.
45 David Lynch and Kristine McKenna, *Room to Dream* (New York: Random House, 2018), 82.
46 *Mysteries of Love: The Making of Blue Velvet*, Blue Velvet, DVD, 2002.
47 Chion, *David Lynch*, 23.
48 Chion, *David Lynch*, 44–5.
49 Olson, *Beautiful Dark*, 33.
50 Lynch and McKenna, *Room to Dream*, 83.
51 Lim, *David Lynch*, 38. This is notable because Lynch often makes sounds from other things so that a crying baby comes from a heavily processed monkey sound, for example, and because he often refuses to reveal his sound sources.
52 Chris Rodley, "The *Icon* Profile: David Lynch (1997)," in *David Lynch: Interviews*, ed. Richard A. Barney (Jackson: University Press of Mississippi, 2009), 187.
53 Amy Charlotte McGill, "The Contemporary Hollywood Film Soundtrack: Professional Practices and Sonic Styles Since the 1970s" (Ph.D. Dissertation, University of Exeter, 2008), 126.
54 Hughes, *The Complete Lynch*, 15.
55 Kaleta, *David Lynch*, 9.
56 Hughes, *The Complete Lynch*, 23.
57 "Interview with Alan Splet," *Cagey Films*, December 17, 1981, accessed March 1, 2019, https://web.archive.org/web/20121201060512/http:/www.cageyfilms.com/links/eraserhead/interviews/other-eraserhead-crew/alan-splet/.
58 Alexandra von Stosch, "The Story of Time and Space Concepts—of Reality in the Work of John Cage and David Lynch," in *David Lynch: The Art of the Real* Conference Proceedings, Braunschweig, 2016, eds. Thomas Becker, Wolfram Bergande, Alexandra v. Stosch, and Valeska Schmidt-Thomsen, accessed January 26, 2019, http://lynchconference.hbk-bs.de/the-story-of-time-and-space-concepts-of-reality-in-the-work-of-john-cage-and-david-lynch/.
59 von Stosch, "The Story of Time and Space Concepts."
60 Chion, *David Lynch*, 23. Room tone is the sound that emanates from an open space such as room.
61 Lynch quoted in Stuart Samuels, *Midnight Movies* (New York: Collier Books, 1983), 168.
62 Lynch and McKenna, *Room to Dream*, 73.
63 Annette Davison, "'Up in Flames': Love, Control, and Collaboration in the Soundtrack to *Wild at Heart*," in *The Cinema of David Lynch: American Dreams, Nightmare Visions*, eds. Erica Sheen and Annette Davison (London and New York: Wallflower Press, 2004), 127; Ric Gentry, "Alan Splet and Sound Effects for *Dune*," *American Cinematographer* (December 1984): 62–72.
64 Chion, *David Lynch*, 14; Paul A. Woods, *Weirdsville USA: The Obsessive Universe of David Lynch* (London: Plexus Publishing, 2000), 15.
65 Gentry, "Alan Splet and Sound Effects for *Dune*," 62–3.
66 See, for example, Noel Murray, "Subverting the Classic Score: *The Elephant Man/Dune/The Straight Story*," in *Beyond the Beyond: Music from the Films of David Lynch*, eds. J. C. Gabel and Jessica Hundley (Hat and Beard Press, 2016), 80; Gentry, "Alan Splet and Sound Effects for *Dune*," 63.
67 Andreas Halskov, "'My Dog Barks Some': Animalistic Sounds and Motifs in the Works of David Lynch," *25 Years Later Site*, October 20, 2017, accessed September 15, 2018, https://25yearslatersite.com/2017/10/20/my-dog-barks-some-animalistic-sounds-and-motifs-in-the-works-of-david-lynch/.
68 Halskov, "'My Dog Barks Some.'"
69 Kaleta, *David Lynch*, 9.

70 Emmanuelle Bobée, "Monde 'réel' et monde imaginaire. Le rôle de la bande son dans *Eraserhead*, de David Lynch," *Entrelacs* 8 (2011), accessed December 1, 2018, https://journals.openedition.org/entrelacs/236.
71 Ricardo Sampino Mattarelli, *David Lynch: Sound Designer* (Falconara Mattima: Edizioni Crac, 2014), 35.
72 K. George Godwin, "*Eraserhead* by David Lynch," *Film Quarterly* 39, no. 1 (1985): 37.
73 Chris Rodley, ed. *Lynch on Lynch*, rev. ed. (London: Faber and Faber, 1997), 72–3.
74 For more on the use of electricity in *Twin Peaks: Fire Walk with Me*, see Brooke McCorkle, "There's Always Music in the Air: Sound Design in *Twin Peaks: The Return*," *Musicology Now*, December 12, 2017, accessed October 27, 2020, http://www.musicologynow.org/2017/12/theres-always-music-in-air-sound-design.html.
75 Richard B. Woodward, "Snapping, Humming, Buzzing, Banging: Remembering Alan Splet," *The Paris Review*, May 13, 2014, accessed October 1, 2018, https://www.theparisreview.org/blog/2014/05/13/snapping-humming-buzzing-banging-remembering-alan-splet/.
76 Woods, *Weirdsville USA*, 19.
77 Halsall, *The Films of David Lynch.*
78 Phipps, "Industrial Soundscapes," 86.
79 "Interview with Alan Splet."
80 Stephen Saban and Sarah Longacre, "*Eraserhead:* Is There Life After Birth?" (1977), in *David Lynch: Interviews*, ed. Richard A. Barney (Jackson: University Press of Mississippi, 2009), 4.
81 Saban and Longacre, "*Eraserhead*," 4.
82 Gary Indiana, "Good Eraserhead: Indiana," (1980), *David Lynch: Interviews*, ed. Richard A. Barney (Jackson: University Press of Mississippi, 2009), 10.
83 Phone interview with Dean Hurley, May 21, 2021.
84 McGill, "The Contemporary Hollywood Film Soundtrack," 225.
85 Slavoj Žižek, *The Art of the Ridiculous Sublime: On David Lynch's Lost Highway* (Seattle: Walter Chapin Simpson Center for the Humanities, 2000), 47.
86 Greg Hainge, "Weird or Loopy? Specular Spaces, Feedback and Artifice in *Lost Highway*'s Aesthetics of Sensation," in *The Cinema of David Lynch: American Dreams, Nightmare Visions*, eds. Erica Sheen and Annette Davison (London and New York: Wallflower Press, 2004), 138.
87 Saban and Longacre, "*Eraserhead*," 6.
88 Lynch identifies this scene in his *Masterclass*. See David Lynch Teaches Creativity and Film, "Sound Design and Scoring," *Masterclass*, May 2019, https://www.masterclass.com/classes/david-lynch-teaches-creativity-and-film/chapters/sound-design-and-scoring.
89 Indiana, "Good Eraserhead," 14.
90 Saban and Longacre, "*Eraserhead*," 4.
91 Indiana, "Good Eraserhead," 14; Phipps, "Industrial Soundscapes," 86.
92 Hainge, "Weird or Loopy?," 138.
93 Todd McGowan, *The Impossible David Lynch* (New York: Columbia University Press, 2007), 35.
94 McGill, "The Contemporary Hollywood Film Soundtrack," 126.
95 Woods, *Weirdsville USA*, 19.
96 Kenneth George Godwin, "Interview with David Lynch, December 1981," in *Eraserhead: The David Lynch Files: Volume 1*, Kenneth George Godwin (Orlando: Bear Manor Media, 2020), 155.
97 Godwin, "*Eraserhead* by David Lynch," 37.

98 Jordan, “Starting from Scratch,” 27.
99 McGowan, *The Impossible David Lynch*, 37.
100 Alexander, *The Films of David Lynch*, 21.
101 *Mysteries of Love: The Making of Blue Velvet*, Blue Velvet DVD.

2 Sound Design

As the last chapter discussed, few would argue that among American directors, David Lynch has made movies with some of the most distinctive sounds, which has given rise to the adjective "Lynchian." The director known for films that channel the uncanny and the weird is meticulous about his films' sounds, not only by writing his intended sounds into the script but also by creating the sounds in collaboration with a professional sound designer. He has noted that his scripts are just guides:

> A script is for getting the ideas down, but it's not the final thing at all. It's to remind you of the idea, which could be much fuller than what the words actually are saying. For instance, the script has no sound to it. It's just ideas.[1]

But what exactly are ideas? Robert Sinnerbrink defines ideas for Lynch as "visual and aural sequences that combine images and sounds liberated from a purely narrative function with those evincing a complex cinematic reflexivity" that "disrupt narrative and representational codes, evoking simultaneously pre-representational sensation and self-conscious reflection upon the nature of film."[2] These ideas give rise to the Lynchian sound.

The Lynchian sound is wide-ranging, yet still distinct in terms of its sources, which range from water bottles to songs by well-known bands. Lynch's music and sound do serve a narrative purpose, even if it is not immediately obvious. As I discussed in the previous chapter, Lynch thinks about sound through intuition and experimentation. In this chapter, I will examine the combination of intuition, knowledge, skill, and creativity that fuse together to make the sound design of a Lynch film.

Lynch is best known for his sound design and has redefined the sound world in film through his sound-consciousness.[3] He brings his unique sound to the fore more than any other director.[4] Randy Thom, sound designer for *Wild at Heart* (1990), observed that it would be impossible for Lynch to "do a film with an uninteresting soundtrack if he tried, just because that's the kind of brain he has."[5] Dean Hurley similarly remarked that "David has made an

DOI: 10.4324/9781003265450-2

incredible world for the ears."[6] Lynch, discussing the importance of sound in his works, recounted to Jonathan Sanger, producer of *The Elephant Man* (1980): "Everybody thinks sound is just an addition to the images. Boy, are they wrong about that. Sound is an equal partner and needs to be treated just as specially."[7] One would be hard pressed to disagree that Lynch's films have a sonic awareness not ordinarily found in film.[8]

While Lynch has always been interested in sound, he did not always have this interest. He has mentioned that composer Angelo Badalamenti got him fascinated with music:

> Before that, I loved sound. I loved abstract sound and I loved sound for pictures and film. And I loved to experiment with sound so it sort of fed in. You know, cinema inspires so many different mediums and it was kind of a natural thing but sort of a thing that was quite, as you say, quiet. But going from sound to more abstract sound going into music in an experimental way was the thing.[9]

As I showed in the last chapter, Lynch established his sound design in his early short films and *Eraserhead.* John Alexander has noted that "Lynch's films abound with aural motifs as well as visual; the industrial sounds accompanying images of steam and vapor in *The Elephant Man*; the striking match in *Wild at Heart*, a splashing drop of water in *Dune*."[10] Lynch tends to take these sonic motifs and either doubles or multiplies them, creating a sort of sonic doppelgänger.[11] These sonic markers lie at the heart of Lynch's films, in some cases becoming the hallmark sounds we associate with his films. Sometimes there can be confusion about what a sound is meant to be; for example, in *The Elephant Man*, Anne Coates mistook the sound of raindrops for gunshots due to their excessive volume and emphasis.[12]

Crediting is important for us to understand Lynch's role in his films' sound design, providing a window into exactly what he did to execute, produce, record, mix, remix, and create his films' sounds. Lynch is credited as sound designer and sound re-recording mixer for *Inland Empire*, while Dean Hurley is credited as production sound mixer, sound supervisor, and sound re-recording mixer. This means that Lynch, not Hurley, created the sound design, but both he and Hurley were responsible for the later re-mixing of any sounds during post-production.

Moreover, Lynch considers himself more than the director of his films; he considers himself their sound man.[13] It is not only the use of sound, but it is also how he uses it. As Murray Smith has suggested,

> what makes Lynch's approach so distinctive is the degree to which all elements of sound—score and dialogue included—are subordinated to an integrated sound design, in contrast to the relative autonomy retained by music, dialogue and effects in occasional sound design.[14]

It is from this point that this chapter departs.

To better understand the Lynchian sound, we must understand how he creates and conceives of sound. Dean Hurley, who has worked closely with the director in creating, recording, and mixing his films, has documented how Lynch works in creating sound:

> David was doing everything and it was typically just me serving a wide variety of audio-based roles, and most importantly it was an arena where he didn't differentiate between music or sound. … [which] were considered the same in a lot of ways. I started to realize, under David, the entire creative endeavor of constructing a motion picture experience, sonically, doesn't have to be as complicated as it is for the larger projects with committees of producers, test screenings and strict schedules.[15]

Thus, Lynch functions as the sound designer in his films much more than the people he employs to work on sound. While Lynch's sound design often *sounds* complex, typically it is not. Lynch does not always differentiate between what is music and what is sound design, which explains the frequent blurring between them. We see a similar blurring between non-diegetic and diegetic music, which I will discuss in the next two chapters.

While vague about the meanings of his films, Lynch often talks about his process of and approach to sound design. During a 2010 presentation in Goslar, Germany, when receiving the Kaissering Award, he perfectly encapsulated his approach to sound design:

> To me, there's what you hear is specific sound effects like footsteps, and then there's abstract sound effects, that approach music and they make a mood and then there's music. So, more often than not, the sound comes after the picture. So, if you see a room, and it's completely quiet, you've shot that room and a person's walking, and the light is perfect, the walking is perfect, what the person says over in the corner in the shadow is perfect. But now, you can get some soft footsteps going on the carpet, you can get some feeling from outside and you say, oh I want a wind or some traffic sound or something and you put it in and it completely ruins the mood. So you look for some abstract sound that will give that feeling. And it's an experiment. You might have an idea, you try it, and it's close but then you have to start tweaking it. So you get the sound to marry—I say to marry—to the picture like man and wife. Boom, they're married. And it feels correct. And then there's sometimes many, many sound effects going at once, but conjuring a correct mood and specific sounds that go with the picture and then music is a thing that can come in and give it a mood or it can give an emotion, and so it's very powerful as something you hear. But it has to marry to the picture and that's the tricky thing. It's a feeling like

> you've got many, many, many red lights and suddenly the lights go green and you say, that feels right.[16]

From this, we can understand Lynch's thought process as he determines his films' sound design. Sound consists of multiple layers in each soundtrack.[17] He typically plans sound to function as a portal between the multiple worlds in his films.[18] However, in many cases, as Andrew Burt has observed regarding *Fire Walk with Me*, "the sound design uses everyday diegetic sounds in ominous ways."[19] In this chapter, I discuss the kinds of sounds that Lynch uses in his films and how he typically uses them.

Sound in Script

Lynch's deliberate use of sound design can be seen in his script directions, which in some cases are very clear instances of his intentions, even if they are not heard that way. It is important to remember that Lynch, like all directors, does not indicate all intended sound effects in a script, so the ones not specified in the script should not be discounted as less important than those that are indicated. However, the choice to include certain sound descriptions can help us decipher what Lynch thought about how sound should work in the film.

Although the sounds are often described in the script, Lynch still must work with his sound designers to interpret them, which can be difficult, as Dean Hurley recounted:

> What surprises me as somebody who works for him [is that] my whole MO is to try to align all my sensibilities with his so I can recognize things that will work and I can see things through his eyes. The big example that I always use is this. This struck me like when I first started working for him. A lot of our conversations were about music, [and] he would tell me the kinds of things that he liked. There's a lot of overlap, like a lot of things that we both like, but I remember early on him saying how much he loves ZZ Top. At the time, ZZ Top represented to me an engineer with the way the record sounded, what they embodied. I wasn't on the ZZ Top page. That was one of the only things early on where I didn't see how that was cool because ZZ Top to me seemed really hokey and overproduced rock. Over time, [Lynch] was always asking me to analyze "Sharp Dressed Man," or some of the other songs like when I was learning about them, especially when I would go to play certain things. "Sharp Dressed Man" is kind of like a Texas shuffle rhythm, which sounds like a 4/4 rhythm. But it's not like I was trying to reverse engineer to figure out how to play some of these things because he kept referencing them and wanted to pull in influences, but it never had an appeal to me. But then, in *The Return*, the way it's used is such a unique flavor. All of a sudden, there was some point before *The Return* where my mind flipped over. There's an

> example of David Bowie's "Let's Dance." I was reading some interview at one point and David Bowie was like, "Yeah, I wanted to do like, a Little Richard type song." And he frames, "Let's Dance" like a Little Richard type [song]. But you can hear it in the intro. And it hit me like that's what that caliber of artist is seeing. They're seeing a bit of the future. He's going after the things that he was enthusiastic [about], whereas I would [say] "you want a Little Richard, so we should probably focus on like a piano bass Boogie Woogie." An artist is giving me clues on what their influences are and what they want to try to do. I would go at face value but I think it's the way these things hit them, and they end up going at it in a different way. So finally, one day, it just hit me the way David saw ZZ Top: it's the blues. But it's this hyper stylized, almost like chrome-plated, futuristic version of the blues. And once I saw it from that angle, I was like, I can understand this.[20]

As we can see from the script directions and Hurley's account, deciphering Lynch's intentions for sound is not always easy. Another example is when Lynch told Hurley "to put the John Lennon sound on it."[21] Hurley explained:

> The John Lennon sound for him is definitely a vocal echo effect. It's, like, a 114 or 112 millisecond flap delay, and then mixing in a little bit of something they invented for John Lennon, which was called the ADT, the automatic double-tracking. The engineers at Abbey Road had to basically pull this technique out of thin air with micro-delays to make it, because he loved the sound of his voice double-tracked.[22]

As I will discuss in Chapter 5, vocal effects, especially those using processing and echo, are heard frequently in Lynch's works, creating a standard sound of the voice in his films, similar to the "John Lennon sound" to which Hurley referred. Lynch considers sound as creating a world; it allows him to establish environment in a way differently than just using visuals. John Neff has corroborated Hurley's observations on working with Lynch and his emphasis on creating sound:

> David of course is very hands-on in the sound department. He is the sound designer for the movie. He conceptualizes things and says, "I need it to sound like a 30-ton piece of metal being scraped across a polished piece of smooth granite." Well, you have to imagine in your mind how that's gonna sound, then you have to go make it out of things that exist in the everyday real world. But he directs, he's an act and react guy. You come up with something you think might get you started on that path and then he goes, "OK, no, it's gotta be lower, it's gotta be slower, it's gotta have this, more reverb." So he directs the creation of the sound like he directs the picture.[23]

What emerges is that Lynch has sounds that he likes, and while he may not be able to specify them in technical terms, he alludes to them, and their incorporation becomes a pervasive feature throughout his works.

He also includes recording effects such as echoes in his scripts. In *Lost Highway*, echoes pervade the soundscape as Fred Madison (Bill Pullman) traverses the hallways of his house before he sees the reflection of the Mystery Man (Robert Blake) in the mirror. In *Mulholland Drive*, echoes are reserved for footsteps which, in this context, makes the room sound larger than it looks.[24] We can also see the role of echo effects in the script of *Dune*, which appear throughout, not just as effects but as functional sounds.

Noise vs. Sound

In this chapter, I adopt Philip Halsall's distinction between noise and sound in which noise "is a sound such as a bang, drip or crash," while sound "is the umbrella-like term that covers music, noise and dialogue in much the same way that image covers painting, film or photograph."[25] Lynch strategically employs both in his sound design and uses each differently depending on his goals for the film. In this way, he creates a unique audioscape for every film he directs. Michel Chion believes that in Lynch's films "sound is the very origin of certain images. A character hears someone or something and this brings on visions."[26] For instance, as Martha Nochimson writes about the ceiling fan in *Twin Peaks,*

> the sound design encourages us to listen to the air churning loudly through the fan's revolving blades in a new way. The air is a counterforce, a power already there before the fan begins to move, made more visible and audible by the human made machine.[27]

This is a product of how Lynch uses sound in the narrative. Greg Hainge lists three quintessential elements of Lynchian cinema, and two of them—electricity and noise—are sonic, while the third—light—is visual.[28] Lynch remarks that sound "is a concrete and powerful entity which physically inhabits the film."[29]

It is unsurprising that Lynch's films are often described as noisy.[30] Annette Davison describes noise in his films as "sounds with a high proportion of inharmonic spectral components."[31] Often the places the script describes as noisy are also described as devoid of meaning, with the noises functioning as space-fillers.[32] However, this contention is inaccurate as the noises clarify the mood and ambience of the scene.[33] Like sound, noise can be either diegetic or non-diegetic. Chion considers Lynch's films noisy because "he makes eager and frequent use of the violent intensity contrasts that modern sound makes possible in cinema."[34] But Hurley has explained this noisiness by describing Lynch's use of sound as a collision of elements.[35] Sometimes deciding whether something is noise or sound can be difficult.

Sound effects—especially in the context of *The Return* (which David Lynch conceived as an 18-hour film rather than a television serial, despite its airing in 18 parts on the Showtime television network)—not only disorient the viewer but also function as portents. Remarkably, an X (formerly Twitter) bot exists that tweets screen grabs from *The Return* every hour with the closed captioning of the sound effects (Figure 2.1), which illustrates the importance of sound in the series.[36] These captions are carefully considered, from the "electrical pop" when Cooper-as-Dougie puts the fork in the outlet to the "wind whooshing" outside the Double R Diner to the "machine chiming wildly, alarm blaring" as Cooper-as-Dougie wins one jackpot after the other in the Silver Mustang casino. Andrew T. Burt observes that "sound is often manipulated, distorted, and various motifs are endlessly reconfigured and changed to disorient, confuse, and reconfigure audience expectation."[37] In *The Return*, sound design plays a doubly important role. Since there is far less music than in the first two seasons of *Twin Peaks*, or even in Lynch's other films, the sound design must function as the music would to compensate for the dearth of music.[38] But noises, on the other hand, tend to function throughout Lynch's films as leitmotifs, such as the gaslight flames and the hissing steam in *The Elephant Man*.[39]

Lynch's sound effects tend to go unnoticed because of his skill in combining music and sound effects.[40] The boundary is often blurred and sometimes it is difficult to tell where the music ends and the sound effects begin; as Lynch says, "I really like the idea of sound effects being used as music."[41] For this

Figure 2.1 Screen Grab from *The Return* Illustrating the Captioning of Sound

reason, especially in his earliest films, the sound effects function as musical underscore where music might occur instead. Lynch felt that the image should not be given primacy over the audio track, which includes sound effects, music, and dialogue.[42]

Noise and sound differ in Lynch's films, and both are equally important. We can make some general statements about the differences in how Lynch's films employ them. Halsall defines the use of noise and sound in Lynchian aesthetics:

> Sounds are not only incorporated into the web of the film in order to create the reality of that era, but they are over-emphasized so that the noise, not the musical score, creates a soundtrack, although both are used to great effect.[43]

Therefore, noise works in tandem with the sounds to create the soundtrack, one that creates what Halsall calls an audio narrative comprised of three key elements—background noise, silence, and dialogue—that work both separately and together to accomplish this narrative.[44] But it is also the difference in how noise and sound function. Noise typically serves as a sonic interrupter, often in quiet places.[45] Sound serves to create an environment.

Hainge categorizes noise in Lynch's films as not only pervasive and wide-ranging but also as sounds that "seem constantly to dissolve into the noise from which they are constituted, both philosophically and formally, to erase their own form and identity or, perhaps, the possibility of imposing on them anything that would resemble a form, identity, or meaning."[46] He reads *Eraserhead* as a noisy film due to the transgression of sonic boundaries.[47] These sonic transgressions, of course, are not limited to *Eraserhead* but also occur in many of Lynch's other films. Lynch uses noise abstractly, often in a haunting fashion, specifically with low-frequency noises that also combine with other sounds that can "create atmospheres of disquiet and liminality."[48] Although various specific sounds can have low-frequency noises, they are usually associated with abstract ambient sounds that are meant to displace and discomfort viewers.

Regardless of whether what we hear in a Lynch film is sound or noise, it remains that Lynch used low tones as part of the sound design early in his career, but more recently he has used higher sounds. He has also tended to reserve sound effects for moments of fear, horror, or intense mood.[49] Lynch's noise and sound sources come from a variety of places, but most often as a combination of both organic and inorganic places.[50] For this reason, they do not always sound like the source from where they are supposed to be emanating. This kind of sound mismatch notably occurs in the opening scene of *The Return*.

One sound that is what it seems is white noise. White noise is a characteristic sound in Lynch's films; the way he uses it is one of his sonic hallmarks, and it typically is associated with abstract sound. As Isabella Van Elferen writes,

> Since it lacks rhythm, melody, and harmonic progression, timbre is the only actual quality of the white noise that is Lynch's foremost sonic trademark. His soundtracks are conceived as thick textures in which acoustic sounds are mixed into the background and made fuzzy by an overlay of white noise. The timbre of this white noise can best be described by metaphors of air blowing through metal pipes, or the whirring of electrical cables, or the sound of wind in trees. It travels through all the diegetic, extra-diegetic, and meta-diegetic timespaces of his films.[51]

White noise, therefore, is a core component of Lynch's soundtracks, often having its timbral sound present even when it is difficult to hear. Van Elferen notes that white noise is such a characteristic Lynchian sound that it can be heard even during the menu screen showings of his DVD films.[52]

As we have seen in various examples, Lynch's films are pervaded with low-end sounds. Sometimes these low sounds are confined to environmental noise or room tone, and sometimes as drones, while in other cases they function as characters on their own. In films that use industrial sounds, like *Eraserhead* and *The Elephant Man*, low-end sounds sometimes provide a white noise effect.[53] We can see this at least once in each of his films. For example, the low sounds occur in *Dune* as rumbles that indicate the presence of the sandworms, of which Lynch noted: "The sound of them alone will bring you to your knees."[54] *Dune* has been said to be the film with the lowest sounds in all of Lynch's works, likely due to its extraterrestrial environment.[55]

But music and sound are not always clearly differentiated. As Steven Wilson contends, underscoring in Lynch's works should not be relegated to the traditional definition of music. Rather, "Lynch's work requires a broader understanding that includes drones and aestheticized ambient sound."[56] Wilson makes a tripartite distinction for Lynchian sound: "dramatic ambient sound, conventional underscoring, and motivic sound."[57] Therefore, we can consider how each of these categories works. Ambient sound is typically confined to sound effects that occur in an environment, usually diegetic. Conventional underscoring is the use of non-diegetic music cues used to highlight important or dramatic moments, including sound bridges. Motivic sound is a subset of both conventional scoring and sound effects, and it falls under the guise of leitmotifs or recurring themes to represent people, places, or events. Wilson, however, does not account for diegetic or source music, which I argue is a fourth layer in Lynch's films.

Human Sound vs. Non-human Sound

While Lynch's unique use of sound effects has never been overlooked, their categorization sometimes has been. In addition to determining whether something in a Lynch film is sound or noise, we can divide those in the sound category into human or non-human sound.[58] Human sounds tend to come from people but, as we know with Lynch, sometimes this is not so simple. Non-human sounds are often industrial sounds or electricity sounds; they can also be sounds related to nature, including animal sounds. I will discuss the typical human sounds he uses in detail in Chapter 5 as they correlate with the voice.

Non-human sounds take a variety of shapes in Lynch's works. They serve to create ambience, clarify environment, and disorient the viewer. Sometimes, as I will discuss in Chapter 5, they involve the human voice making animal sounds. But more often they include multiple sounds that are processed and overdubbed with other sounds to create an entirely new sound. This is evident in his use of nature sounds such as wind, the sounds of electricity and static, and industrial sounds. However, if we return to Wilson's tripartite division of the Lynchian sound, and the notion that music and sound cannot always be clearly demarcated, we can see that sometimes electricity, static, and industrial sounds can function as leitmotifs. This can be seen in many of Lynch's films, but especially in *Fire Walk with Me, The Elephant Man,* and *Eraserhead.* However, these sounds often fall into another category: environmental sounds.

Environmental Sounds

For Lynch, sound creates a world, but there are some films in which this is acutely true, given that they occur in distant places, alternate universes, or fantasy worlds. One example of this is *Dune.* For *Dune*, the sound had to create a world far more interesting than one would find in a typical Lynch film because it was set on the planet Arrakis. To create some of the worlds in his films, Lynch relies on aural motifs such as the sound of water droplets in *Dune* but also the steam sounds in *The Elephant Man* and the sounds of industry in *Eraserhead.*[59] It was important for Lynch to establish that the filmic environment in the former was in nineteenth-century England and the latter in twentieth-century Philadelphia, so the soundscapes were crucial to the storytelling. This use of specific kinds of sound to establish place creates an aural consistency and helps create a world both sonically and visually. This use of single sonic motifs in each of these films to create aural landscapes is one reason why Tim Hewitt has stated that these films are bound together in a consistent sonic style.[60]

In *Dune*, sound is not only ambient and world-creating; it is also functional. For instance, as Michel Chion notes, "vibrations are used to lure the sandworms, and a magic voice to paralyze the enemy."[61] These all occur as a way to establish the film's location. As was typical for the creation of otherworldly environmental sounds, these sounds were made through manipulating and combining traditional sounds. The sandworms sound was created by combining, processing, and reprocessing a mixture of four animal sounds: horse, pig, baboon, and puma.[62] As the worms move, they create an otherworldly rumble made from unconventional sources. Alan Splet explains:

> I again combined several things. Some of it is made from bomb blasts that I took from the library and slowed down about five or six times. Then, Ann [Kroeber, Splet's wife and sound partner] went out with a Frap [type of microphone] and bonded it to a piece of plexiglass in the sand at a playground and did all sorts of things to it, rubbing and scraping sand over the top of it, scraping it, dragging it. I used almost everything she got. I processed that through the phlanger in places and the harmonizer in others. It came out well, like a mild earthquake traveling under the desert.[63]

As was typical, Splet began recording and processing sounds even before pre-production began, using the script to guide him in creating the three sound worlds, one for each planet:

> First was Caladan, home of the Atreides family, a kind of replica of earth, fertile and lush. Then there was Geidi Prime, a grotesque mechanical world of rails, steam, metal and petroleum spills, where the malevolent Harkonnens originate. And then Arrakis, the desert planet, arid and stormy, otherwise known as Dune.[64]

For Arrakis in particular, Splet made the dry desert winds audible to the listener, though there were also dry desert winds on the other two planets.[65]

Sound Design and Collaborations

In this chapter, I will not consider in depth the composers with whom Lynch worked but only the sound designers: Alan Splet, Randy Thom, and Dean Hurley. I will also briefly discuss Ann Kroeber, Splet's widow, who recorded many of Lynch's sound effects. I will mention Angelo Badalamenti, but only in the context of the intersection between music and sound effects. As I mentioned in the previous chapter, Lynch's early forays into sound design were with Bob Collum, but he soon worked with Splet, as early as *The Grandmother*. *Dune* (1984) was the last film on which Splet would collaborate with Lynch. After *Dune*, Lynch often worked alone on his films' sound design, except for with *Wild at Heart* when he worked with Randy Thom, until he began to collaborate with Hurley shortly before *Inland Empire* (2006). However, his collaborations with Hurley did not mean he returned to the same kind of working relationship that he had with Splet. Rather, he continued to take the upper hand in the creation of sound design, working with Hurley on the technical side of sound creation.

The relationship between Lynch and his collaborators and their role in the creation of his sonic style cannot be understated. Holly Rogers attributes the establishment of Lynch's sonic style to his collaborations with two sound designers during the formative years of his career: Alan Splet and Randy Thom.[66] Lynch often involves his collaborators early in the production—sometimes even during pre-production—and this affords them an extended period of time with which to work on the sound. This pattern began with his collaborations with Splet.[67] *Fire Walk with Me* was Lynch's first film that did not include a collaboration with Splet and, notably, for which Lynch did the sound design alone.[68]

Lynch uses sound effects in a musical way.[69] Lynch once remarked that his interest in sounds always included the ways that sound effects can approach music.[70] Sometimes it is impossible to tell where sound effects and music begin and end, or when the diegetic sounds end and the non-diegetic sounds begin and vice versa, and this was something that began as early as the short films.

First and foremost, the creation of sound stems from what is onscreen. Lynch and Splet together coined the phrase "picture dictates sound," which is a philosophy that the director would continue to follow even after he no longer worked with Splet.[71] His working relationship often involved drawing pictures for Splet rather than having discussions to indicate how he envisioned the film's sound. Lynch outlined the process as taking one sound and adding and subtracting things from it, resulting in "action and reaction until you get what you feel is correct."[72] Lynch did not just make the sounds during post-production; he and Splet also did them before, during, and after the filming.[73] However, there are specific sounds that Lynch and Splet made that are characteristically Lynchian, such as drones.[74] For *The Elephant Man,* Splet brought his own recording equipment to England, "which included a harmonizer, which could change the pitch of a voice or a sound without changing its timing or synch."[75] These sonic manipulations gave the film an uncanny sound that fit with what the viewers were seeing in the recreation of nineteenth-century England onscreen.

Because Splet was otherwise engaged during *Wild at Heart*, Randy Thom worked with Lynch on the film's sound design.[76] This was Lynch's only collaboration with Thom, and we can see how Thom's idea of sound's role affected the film's sound design and how it aligned with Lynch's typical sound design style. In interviews, Thom did not elaborate on his working process with Lynch, but he did mention that Lynch is a "soni-matic" director who uses sound to open the world of the film and its characters to the audience.[77] Lynch uses the kinds of sounds that we equate with his films: industrial, nature-based, and complex, likely due to his direction. We can see this in how the sounds for the film are compiled, edited, and dubbed.

Lynch does work slightly differently with different sound designers, yet still achieving the desired effect. With Splet (and Bob Collum before him), he would go through a sound library to see if there was anything that could be used either as it stood or in combination with effects and then, if they established there was nothing usable, they would create new sounds from scratch. When working with Hurley, Lynch does not think about sound representationally. He also works quickly to manufacture sounds that do not exist in their sound library, similar to what he did with Splet.[78] The difference is that Hurley relies on the information in the script when providing the sound, with Lynch doing a majority of the work.[79] Hurley also works in a similar manner to how Badalamenti works with Lynch, creating sounds based on descriptions and moods that the director provides to him, tweaking them as he deems necessary.

Fast Sound and Slow Sound

In an article for *Film Ireland* (1997), Tony McKibbin describes the use of sound in Lynch's films, specifically that of *Lost Highway*:

> Using a Lynchian vocabulary, we can suggest the first scene utilizes "fast sound"; the latter "slow sound." In fast sound our nerves are often stretched and in slow sound ostensibly assuaged, or at least temporarily relieved from dramatic exigencies and nerve pounding.[80]

This sound use is not altogether unexpected since music in the film tends to offer commentary that supplants any dialogue, so it helps to sonically contextualize the scene.[81] And it is useful to examine the employment of fast and slow sound in Lynch's films and consider the patterns for the use of each type.

Fast and slow sound has nothing to do with rhythm or tempo. Rather, it concerns how sound moves to create an environment and then build and use tension. Typically, the narrative determines whether fast or slow sound is used as well as the speed of the visual elements on the image track. This is clearly done throughout *Inland Empire*. However, sometimes they will not work together. In Part 8 of *The Return*, for example, often there is an opposition between fast motion and slow sound, such as when the woodsmen try to revive Mr. C (Kyle MacLachlan). Films such as *The Elephant Man* are based around slow sounds, but Lynch's abrupt use of fast sounds, typically of industry, serve to heighten the difference between John Merrick's (the elephant man, so-called because of his severe deformity) world and the world around him. For this reason, Lynch's sound speeds present us with the illusion that the sound is either slowly or rapidly emerging from the onscreen images.[82] Sometimes this correlates with what we see on screen but, in cases where Lynch wants to disorient the viewer, he does not correlate sound with image.

Room Tone

As I discussed in Chapter 1, room tone first appears in *Eraserhead.* Lynch is known for using room tone, which he defines as "an uncomfortable buzz of white noise that represents 'the sound that you hear when there's silence, in between words or sentences.'"[83] He uses room tone both in scenes with and without music. Lynch prefers room tones that border on music; in fact, room tone in his films often comes from slowed down pieces of music and organ sounds.[84] More practically, room tone is recorded to ensure that any redubbing is consistent.[85]

We cannot always hear room tone, but it plays an important role in all of Lynch's works. Dean Hurley reads *Eraserhead* as Lynch's first film to use room tone coherently, but he also notes its connection to music:

> That was the subtle example of the *Eraserhead* world where he was bombastically piling on the sound to create this entire world off screen. That early encounter was a bit like sonically painting the walls of every single scene, considering everything. And that's why sometimes he would ask for, in every scene of a film, some sense of room tone. If they're noise reducing, and restricting fluid floor noise of the dialogue production track of a film, you're typically finding some sort of fill or realistic room tone, then put back in a little bit of the breath or air. Otherwise, if you clamp down and you noise reduce everything, it just sounds incredibly sterile, almost like ADR. So he would never ask for it. For him, even the simplest room tone was an opportunity for mood. Oftentimes, he would ask for things like an organ room tone, where it would be like a room tone, but there would be a little bit of musicality, a little bit of a harmonic structure; you can hear a lot in *Lost Highway*. There's harmonic content to pretty much every scene, even when music isn't playing. That always struck me as, wow, here's somebody who's micro scoring, even a scene without music. The more obvious example is *Eraserhead* because all that stuff is so foregrounded and so loud and oppressive. But he continues to do it in other films as well. And so there's just this thought that every sonic element brings with it [a] mood or component to lock everything into place.[86]

Hurley makes an important point here: room tone is about creating mood and ambience that cannot be created through standard sound effects. It is a way in which the environment is created both subtly and subliminally for the viewer, but it is not, however, simply a drone or a low-end sound.

Room tone is typically associated with *Inland Empire*, but as Hurley noted, we encounter it as early as *Eraserhead* and even in Lynch's short films. Room tone features prominently throughout *The Return.* The room tone found throughout most of the series comes from one source: the sound of the air duct in the motel room where they filmed the scenes in question. Hurley said that the room tone was

> very faint but it sounded like this harmonic, almost choral sound. You could hear only the faintest suggestion of it, but I thought it sounded very interesting. I comb-filtered it to dial up the specific frequencies that would exaggerate the sound that the tone was harmonizing at. … [It was a] music-esque room tone that was incredibly rich in mood.[87]

Hurley constantly manipulated that one tone throughout the work; in one scene he "automated the comb filter parameters to have them start rubbing against each other to create more of an unsettling *disharmony*."[88] This notion of "disharmony" is not only a core aspect of room tone; it is also a core aspect of many Lynchian works.

Specific Sound Effects

While Lynch can be vague when describing what he wants in sound, sometimes he can also be strangely specific. Lynch often mentions two types of sound effects in his works: specific sound effects (also called hard effects) and abstract sound effects, and he discusses how he uses them to create an overarching sonic aesthetic.[89] Lynch never differentiates the two, but we can define specific sound effects as those that correlate with an on-screen item, action, or object, such as the slamming of a door or a baby crying, and sound as they should. An abstract sound effect is one that often is a conglomeration of sounds that form a single unrecognizable sound for the sake of creating a mood or atmosphere. Sometimes an abstract sound approximates a sound.

Lynch often describes specific sound effects—or lack thereof—in his scripts, foregrounding them, but sometimes he alters them during post-production if he does not feel they create his desired effect. They play a prominent role in enhancing the narrative and are often meticulously described.[90] For instance, in the script for *Lost Highway* Lynch specifies the use of a droning sound seven times, but without noting what makes the drone.[91] Sometimes, it is all about what the sound is rather that what it is made with; this latter part often comes later unless Lynch knows ahead of time exactly how he wants sounds to be made.

Although the sounds in a Lynch film may come from sources other than what they are meant to evoke—such as the sound of Frank Booth (Dennis Hopper) hitting Dorothy Vallens (Isabella Rossellini) in *Blue Velvet* (1986), made by striking a dried-out pumpkin with a cork-backed steel ruler, and the sound of the insects on the severed ear, made by using the sound of roaches walking over stretched latex—they are still considered to be specific sound effects though the source does not matter.[92] Ambiguity distinguishes specific sound effects from abstract sound effects. Sometimes this ambiguity comes in the form of unintelligible sounds that parallel the narrative and character development in the film, but sometimes it serves to decenter the viewer. Ambiguity can also create unusual results in cause-and-effect sounds. As Colin Odell and Michelle LeBlanc write:

> Lynch also likes to make use of the representation of sound, in some way a deliberate use of false sounding foley. In many of his films screams don't sound like they do in real life—they are accentuated representations of screams or distorted versions of them. Similarly Lynch uses sound metaphors, particularly animal or industrial noises, to create a greater impact than realistic sound effects.[93]

Lynch often heightens his specific sound effects in context, mainly to create a type of ambiance. Some of his preferred specific sound effects include gramophone or record needles, static, and wind, sometimes in different guises. For instance, the whirring of the ceiling fan in the Palmer residence that features so prominently in the world of *Twin Peaks* can be considered a subset of wind sounds.

But specific sound effects are not always limited to the film proper; often they are used in the opening credits. In *Wild at Heart*, we hear the heavily amplified sound of the striking of a match and the burning of the flame, juxtaposed with the title credit music.[94] Randy Thom has recounted that the sound of the match was made from flares, an explosion, and some of his voice processed. In *Fire Walk with Me,* a staticky television accompanies the opening credits. In *Lost Highway*, we hear the slow burning of a cigarette as the sound of a cabin explosion plays in reverse.[95] Static also forms an integral part of the video cassette noises, along with its requisite glitches, in *Lost Highway.*[96] Odell and LeBlanc call these "sound closeups."[97]

As I noted in Chapter 1, animal sounds were prominent in Lynch's films since *The Grandmother*, and they continue to be a part of his sonic style in his feature films. In films such as *The Straight Story*, they serve as ambient noise, but there are other more sinister uses of them. In *The Return*, animal sounds—specifically the sound of barking dogs—are used to represent madness. Andreas Halskov has outlined the three most frequent uses of animal sounds in Lynch's films: to represent a loss of control, to illustrate the predatory side of a character, and to represent primal urges.[98]

Drones also appear frequently in Lynch's works. In many ways, we can consider Lynch's siren looping in *Six Men Getting Sick* as the first use of a drone in his films. Drones also are frequently used in his films and play an important role in *The Straight Story*, *Inland Empire*, and *Lost Highway.* In the latter, the droning sound is indicated in the script seven times.[99] Sometimes in *Lost Highway* the drone is so subtle that it is almost inaudible. Robert Robertson calls these "drone pedals." He remarks that they function as an indicator of threat, creating suspense. Lynch does not use only one type of drone—some are high-pitched and some low-pitched. White noise can also function as a drone.[100] Drones have also appeared prominently in *The Return* as a way to sonically distract and disorient the viewer. Two examples of this include the mysterious sound emanating from the walls of the Great Northern Hotel and in Gordon Cole's dream of Monica Belushi. As Zeynep Toraman has observed, in the context of the latter, the droning becomes louder and more persistent the farther into the narration of the dream Cole gets, likely representing "his subjective hearing and a reflection of his mental effort."[101] So, sometimes the drones we hear are point-of-view sounds that emanate not from the film's diegesis but from the position of the on-screen character; sometimes it is difficult to tell one from the other.

Like drones and wind, the sound of electricity has played an important role in Lynch's films. Electricity often assumes the role of a character, and Lynch treats it with buzzing and glitches at opportune moments.[102] This, too, derived from the abstract use of sound in such early short films as *Six Men Getting Sick.*[103] Speaking of a recording of electricity that he had made a decade earlier, Hurley noted that for *The Return*: "I knew that if what I had recorded years ago was a 120-pound-person version of electricity, we needed an 800-pound-person version of electricity."[104] He recorded this sound in Poland when the blanket of snow made a unique sound in the power lines and the snow stopped an electrical current, causing a transformer overload.[105] Electricity is often combined with other sound effects, such as wind in *The Return.*[106] But many sound effects in *The Return* originated as musical sounds, partially because electricity does not record very well. Therefore, small sounds that bordered on music made these sounds.[107] Hurley remarked that even when music is not present, there is some musicality to Lynch's sound effects[108] Lynch himself once noted that "there are sound effects, there are abstract sound effects … music turns into sounds, and sounds turn into music."[109] He believes that "the borderline between sound effects and music is the most *beautiful* area."[110] By extension, the crackling sound of a Geiger counter, which indicates the presence of radiation, appears in Part 8 of the series. In *Inland Empire*, the electricity sound comes from placing an electrical hum on a keyboard that Lynch then played.[111]

Industrial or mechanical sounds, whether from a factory in *Eraserhead* or a grain elevator in *The Straight Story* (1999), are pervasive sonic elements in Lynch's films. As composer Marek Zebrowski has recounted, "David loves these places and finds quite a lot of poetry in the visual juxtaposition of old industries overgrown with weeds and ruined interiors and this mysterious atmosphere, you know, these films of the same flavor."[112] For *The Elephant Man,* Splet went out on location to capture sounds such as smoke emanating from smoke stacks.[113] For example, the grain elevator sounds more like thunder and is dubbed in the foreground. Often, these sounds are combined with other sounds, usually wind or nature sounds, to polarize the natural from the mechanical. Sometimes we cannot tell what sound is foregrounded, and this is another way that Lynch plays with sound. Lynch overlays industrial sounds on music in his 1995 short film *Premonition Following an Evil Deed.* This 52-second film was part of a project that involved 41 filmmakers who were each given the Lumière brothers' cinématographe, the first moving picture camera, to record a film. The music in Lynch's contribution sounds like "a warped classic film score on top of the noise of aging machinery."[114] This notion of aging and decrepit machinery is a component of Lynch's works all the way back to *Eraserhead.*

Lynch's love of wind has been well documented, especially recently, and he frequently uses wind sounds in his works.[115] Kroeber recounted that for *Lost Highway* Lynch's office called her and requested "dreamy winds." Because of her collaborations with him through Splet, she knew that "dreamy meant low and lower, it means nightmare dreams."[116] Wind is found in films such as *The Elephant Man* and *Blue Velvet* to enhance the environment or portray the unusual circumstances that a character faces. Sometimes, wind inspires sounds, such as the whooshing sound that Lynch uses in *Mulholland Drive* and *Blue Velvet.*[117] Wind is sometimes used as a way to denote seediness, as we see in *Blue Velvet*, where the sound is audible and combined with industrial noises that emanate from outside of the Deep River Apartments.

Abstract Sound Effects

Abstract sound effects are usually created by combining multiple sounds that do not have any specific referent. Amy McGill calls the abstract sound effects found in Lynch's films unusual and unrealistic.[118] Nevertheless, "the sounds that emanate forge believable ontological relationships with the images they represent."[119] Frank Gaeta, sound editor for *Lost Highway*, remarked that Lynch often described his ideas for abstract sound effects as a kind of feeling or emotion rather than as specific sounds, specifying that he wanted "oppressive" or "ominous" sound effects, for example.[120] As he does with specific sound effects, Lynch often specifies the abstract sound effects in his scripts. His abstract sounds, however, often border on the musical, which is relatively easy to do since so much of his sound design is infused with a sense of musicality.[121] These sound effects are frequently ambient sounds, and they serve to illustrate and subdue the onscreen environment when something is amiss.[122]

Lynch often achieves his abstract sound effects through mixing and combining multiple sounds, often also speeding them up, slowing them down, and/or processing them. Lynch once said that "it doesn't matter what the technology is: it's what the sounds are and how they're mixed together."[123] For example, although he does not specify where, Lynch claims that there is a point in *Wild at Heart* (1990) when he simultaneously uses 25 different sounds.[124] This simultaneous combination of multiple items on the soundtrack is what Kenneth Kaleta says gives the film its wildness.[125] In films such as *Dune,* there were at times 200 tracks on the mixing board at once.[126] While this is an extreme example of how Lynch combines many sounds to create one sound, it does demonstrate that he has very specific ideas in mind of what sound should be and how it should function. This combining of sounds illustrates that while he may intend to portray a specific sound, that specific sound may comprise components of dozens of other sounds.

With Splet, Lynch used everyday objects, often those that were lying around the studio, to create sound.[127] Splet noted that he and Lynch used natural sounds and changed them through processing, often combining them through different devices. But Kroeber specifies that Lynch's sound is all organic and he does not synthesize them; rather, he simply alters and changes them.[128] Splet likened the process to making a stew: "You have a few potatoes, a few peas, some carrots, a little beef. I put it in the pot and taste it every so often to see how it's coming along. Then maybe you need a little more of this or that, and you blend it all together until you get your sound. You know when it's finally right by instinct. It just begins to feel right."[129] Like Lynch, Splet leaned on his instinct when creating sound design, but they both also relied on the script and the cut of the film. This means that although the sound design process often began during pre-production before a single scene was ever shot, they often went back and adjusted the sound once the film had been shot.

Lynch relies more on the sounds made in the studio during post-production than those on the set, which he does not find particularly useful for his purposes. The sounds made on location during shooting (wild recordings) are very rarely the sounds that he uses in the final film.[130] However, other sounds come from field recordings or wild recordings. For *Dune,* Splet recounted, Kroger took a Nagra IV stereo, a Schoeps CMC 4 microphone, and a FRAP contact microphone, along with several other microphones, and went to a Chevron Oil Refinery in Richmond in search of sounds for the planet Geidi Prime:[131]

> Ann took the Nagra and put the mike wherever she thought something interesting was coming from. She mainly went to get heavy steam and possibly oil flowing through pipes. But she actually got some other stuff by what I call "soundman's luck." Lots of things just sort of come our way. One of these was an empty, 50-foot diameter oil tank. Some of the Chevron people were working on it and one of them threw something into the tank as she was going by and it made this great "pinging" sound. So Ann put the contact mike right on the tank and then held a conventional mike in the air as they started to hammer this tank with all sorts of chains and metal bars, kicked it and what have you.' Out of that came weapons for some of the major battle scenes in *Dune*.[132]

The FRAP microphone allowed Splet and Kroeber the chance to hear "inside" of objects, permitting new ways of hearing typical sounds.[133] Lynch was fascinated by the new sonic world that was opened to him through this microphone, and he used the sounds recorded with it as often as he could.

Even before the FRAP microphone was introduced, Lynch was interested in the sounds of the interiors of things. For him, the sounds of the insides of things were far more fascinating than the simple sounds of things; for instance, the sound of a bottle floating in a bathtub was far less interesting and appealing than the sound that same bottle made floating in a bathtub but recorded from the inside. As in *Eraserhead*, the sound design for *Dune* was made, in part, by recording the inside of a giant barrel. Another place that the sounds they recorded for the film was the Pacific Gas and Electric Company where Kroeber and Splet recorded the sounds of exhaust through valves and the humming of electrical currents through wires, and at an unnamed metal refinery where scrap steel was melted in an electric furnace that used 15,000 volts.[134]

At the opening of *Blue Velvet,* the sound of the electrical current is mixed with the sound of the hose on full blast with Tom Beaumont (Jack Harvey) making agonizing noises. Other sounds in the film are dubbed louder than we might expect, such as Double Ed's (Leonard Watkins) seeing-eye stick meeting the floor as he enters the hardware store, the insecticide tank that Jeffrey Beaumont (Kyle MacLachlan) uses inside Dorothy's apartment, the unzipping of Jeffrey's pants as he undresses, Frank's breathing through the oxygen mask, and the sound of Frank using the scissors on Dorothy. But Lynch also alters the sound in specific environments to offset them as special; for example, the sonic profile of Dorothy's apartment changes when Jeffrey enters it. Sometimes this change in sound profile involves moving from a scene with a lot of diegetic or non-diegetic sound to a scene that has no sounds at all, to indicate the significance of the new environment.[135]

A similar sound change happens in *The Straight Story*, between the scene that shows Alvin Straight (Richard Farnsworth) at home and the scene that has him traveling on his riding lawnmower from Iowa to Wisconsin to see his ailing brother Lyle (Harry Dean Stanton). The sounds of the wind and the sprinkler outside the home, at least at the beginning of the film, tend to be dubbed lower and are almost inaudible, emblematic of Alvin's limited, enclosed world. The exception is the sound of the lawnmower, which allows him to break out of that world. This interior loudness begins at the outset of the film, where Alvin's fall inside the house is audible from his neighbor's yard. Further, Lynch uses tonal music when Alvin is on the road, and when Alvin is at home he limits the sounds to ambient sounds, music that lacks resolution, and diegetic source music from radios. This creates a sharp aural contrast.[136]

These abstract sound effects were used as sonic amplification of the visual events. Alan Splet once discussed his use of abstract sound effects, calling it "audio expressionism" in which he amplifies the image track by using sound as interpretation. He noted that "the sound may or may not correspond with the visible movements of things on screen. Instead, it kind of adds to it to create a mood, an atmosphere."[137] Thus, both Lynch and Splet were on the same page when it came to the use of sound as mood. This may be one reason why, in working with later collaborators such as Hurley in sound design and Badalamenti in music, he would describe what he wanted according to a general, overarching mood.

Necessity is the mother of invention, and sound in Lynch's films is no exception to this. Hurley's collaborations with Lynch, like those with Splet, included the creation of sounds due to the lack of available suitable resources. Of some of the sounds in *The Return*, Hurley remarked:

> All this stuff is borne out of specific directives from him, and things that originated on the script level. When I read the script, I was also making notations, because David would very clearly describe things that sound like a distorted jet engine or electricity. Things are also borne out of his ideas, where he would ask for things like "low scary cellos" or "scary choir clusters." And not having a choir available, I would reach for what I had that sounded like that sort of thing. But it's this giant collage of materials that are channeled and funneled ideas that originated with him. I guess it's how the material was speaking to him.[138]

For some of the sound effects, Lynch did not have the specific resources to create his desired sounds. He noted that aside from creating room tone, he created frequency bands, which Hurley described as something that "can give a room rich harmonic content, and then automate frequencies to rub when you want something to go from a pleasant normal to an unsettling discord."[139] This adds another layer to the sound design.

The creation of sound is just as important as the use of sound. Lynch uses what Liz Greene calls "sounds of the past" to aurally manipulate time in films such as *Inland Empire.*[140] This aural manipulation of time also occurs musically in *Eraserhead* with the music by both Fats Waller and the Lady in the Radiator, but in his later films Lynch does this methodically through sound design. Sometimes sounds are used to heighten the reality in a film, not just to illustrate place, and sometimes they function almost spiritually. We see this most clearly in *The Elephant Man.*[141] The combination of the ticking of the clock tower with John Merrick's breathing works together to emphasize the importance of his ability to breathe and illustrates his short time left to live. This breathing is heavily amplified against the other sounds in the film, creating one of the film's repeated sonic motifs.[142]

Abstract sound effects are clearest in *The Straight Story* when we hear combat sounds as Alvin and Verlyn Heller (Wiley Harker) are reminiscing about World War II.[143] We can only recognize them by the context of the conversation; these sounds are aural flashbacks and are only diegetic to the person speaking at the time, and they do not have any specifically identifiable sound with which we can equate them. It is also important to note that many of the abstract sounds in Lynch's films are acousmatic; that is, their source is unable to be located. This is not coincidental as the sonic disassociation through acousmatic sound is connected with the inability to identify the source of the sound, both where it is coming from and what the sound is.

Lynch deliberately employs unintelligible sound effects, blurring the lines between abstract and specific sound effects. An example is in *Mulholland Drive*, when Dan (Patrick Fischler) and Herb (Michael Cooke) pass the dumpster on the side of the restaurant. Andrew Hageman describes this sound as "resembling the auditory sensation of moving through water—an environment once familiar to a human body but left behind at birth, and therefore a sound connected to the repression of one environment when another displaces it."[144] This sound displacement occurs in sound effects that are blurred between specific and abstract sound effects and are strategically placed based on the narrative. This is just another example of how sound is meant to disassociate the viewer.

Cuts and Sonic Segues

Another element of Lynch's sound design concerns how he chooses to cut—or not cut—sound or to segue sound between scenes. This relates to fast and slow sound. These cuts and sonic segues are not simply sound lags or sound advances; rather, they are carefully crafted in a way unique to his work. Writing on *Wild at Heart,* Annette Davison notes:

> Similarly to the music segues, the sonic segues involve movement from a sound in one shot to another in the next shot. More precisely, they usually involve the shift from a sound sourced by one object in one shot to a sound sourced by another in the next. The two sounds are usually physically similar, and it is this sonic isomorphism that forms the bridge between the two, masking the point of juncture.[145]

Further, "there are also many examples of a high degree of integration between the film's sound and music, in which sound effects are used either in combination with, or as segues into or out of, music excerpts."[146] In *Wild at Heart*, as well as in other films, the soundtrack often heightens or minimizes the elisions between cuts through the ways that Lynch places them.

There are different ways that Lynch handles cuts and sonic segues. One of the sonic hallmarks of *Lost Highway* is the frequent cutting between sonically contrasting scenes.[147] Often, Lynch uses music and abstract sounds as he cuts between scenes so that they function as sound bridges. In *The Straight Story*, he uses the drone found in much of the film as a sound segue between Alvin's driving over the Mississippi River Bridge and his arrival at the bar.

Therefore, sound effects such as drones and white noise are used to connect, cut, and bridge scenes.

Volume Levels and Sound Barriers

Along with cuts and segues (and fast and slow sound) there are also sound barriers; that is, one sound blocks the sound of another for narrative purposes. Lynch is also known for his use of contrasting sound levels, often in succession during cuts. He tends to hyper-amplify the sound effect volume to draw the listener into the scene, much to the chagrin of composer Angelo Badalamenti, who often tells Lynch: "No one can leave the theater humming a sound effect."[148] Lynch's penchant for varying volumes comes from his conviction that films must contain sonic contrast.[149] However, Lynch only tends to alter the volume of sound effects, not of music, dubbing the music in his films loudly, as Badalamenti has stated.[150]

Lynch is very meticulous about how his audiences hear his films, and he has often remarked that he does not like the idea of people watching his films on iPhones, or really, any mobile device.[151] But he also exerts control where he can even after production, notably including notes such as those placed in the film canisters sent to theaters requesting that *Mulholland Drive* be played three decibels louder than usual.[152] This, paired with his own use of volume and dubbing, enhances the already amplified sound contrasts in the film. Unfortunately, this becomes lost when we turn on our DVDs and Blu-Rays of *Mulholland Drive*, as we are unable to replicate his request in our own homes, let alone if we watch it on a device such as a tablet. Therefore, in some respects such as this, we are unable to achieve the desired quality that Lynch had in mind for viewers.

This control over sound, not only in style but in volume, is deliberate. As Dean Hurley remarked, "oftentimes, when we're mixing, he always wanted to push [sounds] to be, if something hits hard, he wants to kind of melt your ears—it's just an extreme."[153] In *Blue Velvet*, Lynch dubs the industrial sounds louder, and sometimes he does so outside of the narrative so that they appear to sound random.[154] One example of this is the sound of Jeffrey flushing the toilet that prevents him from hearing Sandy Williams (Laura Dern) beeping the car horn outside that signals Dorothy's return to her apartment. In the script, Lynch specifies that "Jeffrey instinctively has flushed the toilet and because everything else is so quiet the water sounds seem very loud."[155] Although this script notation makes the sound seem as if the louder flushing sound should be naturally occurring, the flushing sound is actually dubbed louder and is thus in the foreground. A similar example of a Lynchian sound barrier is when a specific sound is buried within the mix. This occurs in Part 8 of *The Return* when Ray Monroe (George Griffith) is crying as the woodsmen attempt to revive Mr. C.[156]

Sometimes the varying dubbing levels create the sound barrier. For instance, in *The Straight Story*, Lynch occasionally reduces the volume so that only isolated words, typically in dialogue between Alvin and his daughter, Rose (Sissy Spacek), can be heard, creating a different kind of sound barrier. This happens again toward the end of the film when Alvin is assisted near his brother's home; we cannot hear the exchange clearly between him and the man driving the tractor. What is crucial for sound barriers is that often neither the audience nor the characters can hear what is occurring in the filmic world, but these barriers are still placed strategically.

Sound distortion, too, is important, and we find it throughout Lynch's catalog and in different guises. For example, when speaking of *The Return*, Lynch noted:

> You have a scene in Episode 14 where Sarah Palmer is in a bar and we hear the sound of billiard balls clacking in the background, but they sound distorted. And that, too, fits the reality of what's about to happen, given that Sarah is going to pull her face off. That's like I said, you know, it's tricky business. We were experimenting with some kind of music back there, but when we did, it just draws you out of this scene coming up. There had to be something going in the mix because you see a lot of movement and things happening in the bar when she walks in. But it can't be anything that's going to distract from what's coming up.[157]

Here, we can see Lynch's use of sound distortion to foreshadow onscreen events. But we can also see how the distortion of sound is used to draw the viewer in and out of the scene. Simple sounds, such as those of clacking billiard balls, sound different and odd to us, foreshadowing and replicating the events we are about to see in the bar.

Firewood

One of the sound design terms that Lynch has coined is "firewood," which describes one of the sonic building blocks of his films.[158] While Badalamenti is known for the scores of Lynch's films, he also plays a role in the sound design by creating firewood. Badalamenti describes firewood thusly: "We experimented with some extended techniques and tried creating new sounds with the orchestra on *Lost Highway*. I scored out some long slow, dark string tracks that David would sometimes playback at half speed. We used to call that raw material 'firewood.'"[159] This material would form the basis of some of his ambient sounds in his films.

In email correspondence with me, Badalamenti discussed his working process with Lynch to create firewood:

> All the films and TV (Twin Peaks, etc.) David and I collaborated on, sonically, David would insert what I call drones on the various cues in the project. David asked me to record what he calls firewood, so when we were in recording studios, having access to an orchestra, we would single out the lowest range instruments. For example, 6 basses, bowing on the lowest bass string, contrabass clarinets, 2 or 3 bassoons, lowest tymp[ani] rolls alternating crescendos and decrescendos. We would do a take that would last 15 to 20 minutes long. David would take the mix and half speed it, then takes the half speed and does a quarter speed mix, and he's got his Sonic Firewood.[160]

In another interview, Badalamenti described how Lynch approached the making of firewood specifically during the recording of the score for *Lost Highway* in Prague:

> While we were there David said, "Angelo, I want you to make me some tracks that we'll call firewood that I can use to create sound design. Get some low instruments, like the cello and basses, and record some long, slow passages of music," Badalamenti continued. "I wrote out ten minutes of whole notes and let them sustain to a really slow click track and interspersed it with scratchiness on the bows. When David worked with these slow recordings he'd play them at half speed, sometimes quarter speed. He puts this firewood underneath things, and we've done this a lot."[161]

The creation of firewood emphasizes Lynch's notion that there is a gray area between music and sound effects. Badalamenti has noted Lynch's preferred use of music that is slowed down.[162] Thus, Badalamenti helped Lynch transform music into sound effects. Holly Rogers ascribes this to a Lynchian version of *musique concrète.*[163] As a result, in at least this respect, Badalamenti does have a responsibility for the sound design outside of the musical score, and Lynch often experiments in combining sound effects and music in his films.[164] One example is firewood, which Lynch uses to create a sense of suspense and anxiety and to provide information about characters and unseen events.[165]

Often, firewood is created by taking what Hurley calls buzzwords that Lynch gives him, very similar to the descriptions of abstract sounds, and creating the sound through the manipulation of a pre-existing sound.[166] One of the best examples of firewood came about when Lynch was in Prague recording the score for *Lost Highway*. As John Ross, owner of Digital Sound & Picture, who was responsible for post-production, recounted the process of making firewood:

> He [Lynch] would also divide the orchestra into various components and let them create sounds, like effects, on the instruments. Each player was

> basically given the responsibility to do their own little piece of time—it wasn't an organized event—as a result, it was an interesting cacophony within the orchestra, which we can then use as a color in overlaying another piece of orchestral music. In some sections, we recorded the orchestra the conventional way, as well as directly into containers—two long tubes and a large wine bottle. [Neumann mics were placed inside a large carafe and at the end of long piping tubes, then hung above and behind the conductor.] These sounds were then used to mix in with the orchestra, and we pretty much had no idea how it was going to play. I took sections of the bottle, copied it, looped it, and David used it as an overtone to some of the orchestral pieces. Very difficult to guess how that is going to sound. It has this reedy overtone, which David used as a high-frequency element to sting things with. We might take some of those elements into the workstations and process them and it comes out as a sound effect at the end of the day, or what would traditionally be a sound effect. But it started out as an orchestral piece. So there's a real gray area between what is a sound effect and what is music. We've done things where he's pretty much taken a piece of music, reversed it, dropped it down an octave and played just the reverb return of that.[167]

The recording of firewood lies at the intersection between music and sound effects, often with the line deliberately blurred, but constructed so that they can be combined and manipulated, resulting in abstract sound effects. This is one way that Lynch deliberately reconstructs the role of music to function in multiple ways.

Dean Hurley, too, commented on Lynch's use of firewood, noting that in practice, it borders on both music and sound effects. He stated that although we often do not think of *Eraserhead* as using firewood, especially since it was produced before Lynch started using the term, it actually does: "With *Eraserhead*, he's building this score to raise your head with sound effect firewood, and even using Fats Waller as a little kind of distant sound effect."[168] So, firewood was originally conceived as sound effects but later on was connected to music.

In some ways, we can consider the use of pre-existing sound effects from sound libraries like those that Splet maintained as firewood, which is why we can hear the beginnings of firewood in Lynch's early short films and then later in his feature films. For instance, in *Dune*, not only did Splet create new sound effects; he also used ones that were already in his large 2,000-reel sound effects library, some of which he had used in other films such as *The Black Stallion* (Carroll Ballard, 1979) and *Never Cry Wolf* (Carroll Ballard, 1983). However, as Splet noted, they were so heavily processed and combined with other sources that they were indistinguishable.[169]

Editing Sound

The last thing that should be considered regarding Lynch's sonic style is the role of sound editing. While editing is a traditional part of composing sound in film, Lynch considers editing as having a distinct role. Hurley discussed this in detail:

> Working alongside him for 13 plus years, I often was trying to figure out what makes him tick; that was what made me better. My job is figuring out what he liked, what he responded to, and being able to deliver that stuff. But it was very hard because at the end of the day, I'm still left with the magic image of him that most other people have because it's his relationship to me. He's a music lover and, as a result of that, there's an appreciation for sonics. Because he's spent so much time on it, there's a knowledge of it but so much comes from just the willingness to experiment with things and to try things to see what would happen. He said *The Grandmother*, was an animated film, largely. So he knew he was going to need a ton of sound effects. But when Alan and him started searching through the library, David didn't like anything that he heard. So it's this approach of "I don't like any of this stuff. So we're gonna have to make our own." It's the whole necessity is the mother of invention kind of thing. But the way that we go about it, it'd be sort of a thing where—this was before, Pro Tools, or reverb units, or whatever—they were experimenting with sounds, maybe they had like a library with sound. But they played it through an air duct. And then they had a mike on one end and a speaker on the other to give it a little bit of reverb because they didn't have a plate reverb at whatever facility they were working at, so they did that. But then, listen to it. I think that lies the way that David thinks. Listen back to it and that's interesting: what would happen if we did it again? Taking that sound and playing it again and again. Essentially, it's like [Alvin Lucier's] "I'm Sitting in a Room." You get him stumbling upon that principle and things like comb filtering because of the exaggerated frequencies. All of a sudden that becomes a tool in his toolkit, so the next time it's like I know what that does. Let's take this sound, and I know he can then leap his mind forward. I know what this technique will sound like on this. Let's do that because of this defining of his own practical skills and tools to do this thing. When I started, he was talking at me sometimes in in specific ways, like, "Okay, take that, lower that an octave, play it at half speed but lower the octave below that and double it up with itself." So, you start to see these things like he's done this before and he knows that this is gonna beef up the sound. It's this kind of wonderful way of inventing his own ways of dealing with this stuff. I'm not going to tell you the scene or anything, but there was a scene in *Inland Empire*, nothing too crazy, one of the more

normal themes, and I remember he was just unhappy with something. I don't know what, it just wasn't firing his synapses or tugging at his heart in the way he wanted it to. I remember even at that stage, trying different things, and out of the blue, he said, "What about finding a wind chime for the sea?" I would have never thought of that, but putting a wind chime using it almost like a room tone; it's barely there, but all of a sudden, there's this imperceptible twinkling to the scene and it was different. It just felt different.[170]

As Hurley discussed, Lynch has an acute sense of what can and cannot be edited in the mix: "He just happens to know what he's after but he has a very solid grasp of all the things that can be tweaked. It's definitely the Renaissance approach to it all because there's such prowess between all those different elements."[171] Much of this stems from Lynch's experience in creating sound for his films, but some of it is still intuitive and innovative.

Conclusion

As this chapter has shown, although Lynch worked with several collaborators on his sound design, as well as working alone, there remains an overarching sonic style in Lynch's films, determined by how he uses specific and abstract sound effects and how each is produced and processed. One way that the sound effects function in his films is that an ordinary sound can become frightening in its specific context. This is why sounds that *should* be familiar are not: their context renders them strange.[172] And this creates what Van Elferen deems "the obfuscation of causal relationships between source, sound, and signification" that "engenders cognitive dissonance in audiences, a dissonance that operates in 'the danger zone' of the Lynchian uncanny."[173] With Lynch, sound and vision are often operating as a dissonance.

Davison remarks that the use of sound in Lynch's films form constellations that create sonorous relationships in the film that foreground and background events.[174] These are sounds that work together to create a sense of ambience, but they do not necessarily have to be sounds of the same kind; often, they are not. Sometimes these sounds are formed through the combination of wind, electricity, running water, and footsteps, for example. Typically, Lynch often foregrounds the diegetic sounds in the mix in a way that creates a sense of realism and disassociation at once.[175]

We can, therefore, come to some general conclusions about the sonic style of Lynch's films in terms of sound design and sound effects. There are some commonalities in the ways that the sounds for Lynch's films are made. Large containers are one place in which sounds are often recorded. Lynch uses point-of-view sounds often, and as a result, he sonically manipulates or amplifies them. Sound is also used to create a sense of space, "creating large and cavernous and yet oppressive and claustrophobic spaces."[176] And Lynch uses sound effects as disembodied sounds, in which an obvious source is not visible, serving as vehicles for suspense and audience displacement.[177]

But it is not only the sound types that create Lynch's sonic style, it is also how sound is used, how loud or soft it is, and how it is dubbed. Lynch often uses volume to create a sense of disorientation, with diegetic sounds that are dubbed exactly at the level one might expect, sometimes creating a feeling of voyeurism on the part of the viewer. But he also uses volume as a sound barrier, creating a sense of mystery or to heighten suspense. Volume is also used as part of sound segues and cuts to change the way that sound enters a new scene or departs from one.

There is a sense of sonic evolution in the way that Lynch has used sounds throughout his career. In a 2014 interview, he remarked on the use of sound in his films over the years: "I used to like darkness and low-frequency sounds, and now I tend to go for lighter things and high-frequency sounds."[178] Lynch uses low sounds to indicate danger and fear.[179] We can see this in *The Return* and, in part, in *Inland Empire.* For Lynch, sound often functions as an aural illusion for the viewer, and this has not changed throughout his career. As Dean Hurley noted, sounds often seem to sound bigger than they actually sound.[180]

Ultimately, Lynch constructs his film's sonic style in such a way that the audience must use the sounds to glean their own meanings from them, which is part of what makes the sounds "Lynchian."[181] Regardless of when his films were created and with whom, there is a typical sonic fingerprint in all of Lynch's works. Music is used in a similar manner. In the next two chapters, I will consider how Lynch incorporates both diegetic and non-diegetic music into his sound design and how he uses them in tandem with sound effects.

Notes

1 Ross Simonini, "'Daydreaming Is So Important to Me': How David Lynch Fishes for Ideas," *Art Review*, January 25, 2021, https://artreview.com/daydreaming-is-so-important-to-me-how-david-lynch-fishes-for-ideas/.
2 Robert Sinnerbrink, "*Silencio*: *Mulholland Drive* as Cinematic Romanticism," in *Mulholland Drive*, ed. Zina Giannopolou (London and New York: Routledge, 2013), 80.
3 Kaleta, *David Lynch*, 60; Liz Greene, "Speaking, Singing, Screaming: Controlling the Female Voice in American Cinema," *The Soundtrack* 2, no. 1 (2009): 64.
4 Martha Nochimson, *Television Rewired: The Rise of the Auteur Series* (Austin: University of Texas Press, 2019), 40.
5 Randy Thom, "Designing a Movie for Sound," April 17, 1988, in *Soundscape: The School of Sound Lectures*, 1998–2001, eds. Larry Sider, Diane Freeman, and Jerry Sider (London and New York: Wallflower Press, 2003), 123.

6 Asbjoern Andersen, "Behind the Weird, Wonderful Sound of 'Twin Peaks: The Return' – With Dean Hurley and Ron Eng," *A Sound Effect*, October 4, 2017, accessed February 3, 2019, https://www.asoundeffect.com/twin-peaks-sound/.
7 Jonathan Sanger, *Making The Elephant Man: A Producer's Memoir* (Jefferson, NC: McFarland and Co., 2016), 116.
8 Frances Morgan, "'A Beautiful Trip': An Interview with David Lynch," *The Quietus*, December 12, 2011, accessed March 1, 2019, https://thequietus.com/articles/07565-david-lynch-interview.
9 Jason Bentley, "Interview with David Lynch," KCRW Radio, Los Angeles, January 18, 2011, accessed February 3, 2019, https://www.kcrw.com/music/shows/morning-beomes-eclectic/david-lynch/.
10 Alexander, *The Films of David Lynch*, 21.
11 Kulezic-Wilson, *The Musicality of Narrative Film*, 108.
12 Liz Greene, "*The Elephant Man*'s Sound, Tracked," April 30, 2020, http://www.vimeo.com/413827977.
13 Davison, "'Up in Flames'," 131.
14 Murray Smith, "Theses on the Philosophy of Hollywood History," in *Contemporary Hollywood Cinema*, eds. Steve Neale and Murray Smith (London: Routledge, 1998), 15.
15 Jon Dieringer, "The Frequency of Fear: Dean Hurley Interview," *Screen Slate*, December 7, 2018, https://www.screenslate.com/articles/frequency-fear-dean-hurley-interview.
16 David Lynch, *The Marriage of Picture and Sound*, audio CD, track 3, "The Marriage of Picture and Sound" (Nürnberg: Moderne Kunst Nürnberg, 2012).
17 Martha P. Nochimson, *The Passion of David Lynch: Wild at Heart in Hollywood* (Austin: University of Texas Press, 2012), 36.
18 Scott Wilson, "Neuracinema," in *David Lynch in Theory*, ed. François-Xavier Gleyzon (Prague: Univerzita Karlova v Praze, 2010), 73.
19 Andrew T. Burt, "'The Thread Will Be Torn': Sound Design as a Measure of Self-Knowledge in *Twin Peaks: Fire Walk with Me*," in *The Music of Twin Peaks: Listen to the Sounds*, eds. Reba Wissner and Katherine Reed (Abingdon and New York: Routledge, 2021), 114.
20 Phone interview with Dean Hurley, May 21, 2021.
21 "*Twin Peaks*: An Interview with Music Director Dean Hurley," *Rhino.com*, August 11, 2017, accessed June 1, 2018, https://www.rhino.com/article/twin-peaks-an-interview-with-music-director-dean-hurley.
22 "*Twin Peaks*: An Interview with Music Director Dean Hurley."
23 Mike Smaczylo, "David Lynch and the Surreal Soundscapes of Mulholland Drive," *Muse by Clio,* April 28, 2020, https://musebycl.io/music-film/david-lynch-and-surreal-soundscapes-mulholland-drive.
24 McGill, "The Contemporary Hollywood Film Soundtrack," 271–2.
25 Halsall, *The Films of David Lynch*.
26 Chion, *David Lynch*, 169.
27 Nochimson, *Television Rewired,* 38.
28 Greg Hainge, *Noise Matters: Towards an Ontology of Noise* (New York and London: Bloomsbury, 2013), 185.
29 "A Master Class with David Lynch," in *Moviemakers' Master Class: Private Lessons from the World's Foremost Directors*, ed. Laurent Tirard (New York and London: Faber and Faber, 2002), 128.
30 Liz Greene, "From Noise: Blurring the Boundaries of the Soundtrack," in *The Palgrave Handbook of Sound Design and Music*, eds. Liz Greene and Danijela Kulezic-Wilson (New York: Palgrave Macmillan, 2016), 19–20.

31 Davison, "Demystified, Remystified, and Seduced by Sirens," 142.
32 Greene, "From Noise," 20–1.
33 Greene, "From Noise," 23.
34 Michel Chion, "The Silence of the Loudspeaker, or Why with the Dolby Sound It Is the Sound that Listens to Us," April 16, 1998, in *Soundscape: The School of Sound Lectures*, 1998–2001, eds. Larry Sider, Diane Freeman, and Jerry Sider (London and New York: Wallflower Press, 2003), 153.
35 Daisy Webb, "In Heaven: Celebrating the Surreal Sounds of David Lynch," *Film Daily*, accessed March 1, 2019, https://filmdaily.co/obsessions/the-surreal-sounds-david-lynch/.
36 Kate Ray, *Ominous Whoosh* (@OminousWhoosh), https://twitter.com/ominouswhoosh?lang=en.
37 Andrew T. Burt, "Is It the Wind in the Tall Trees or Just the Distant Buzz of Electricity? Sound and Music as Portent in *Twin Peaks'* Season Three," in *Critical Essays on Twin Peaks: The Return*, ed. Antonio Sanna (New York: Palgrave Macmillan, 2019), 254.
38 Kingsley Marshall and Rupert Loydell, "Sound Design, Music, and the Birth of Evil in *Twin Peaks: The* Return," in *The Music of Twin Peaks: Listen to the Sounds*, eds. Reba Wissner and Katherine Reed (Abingdon and New York: Routledge, 2021), 123.
39 Jeff Smith, "The Auteur Renaissance, 1968–1980," in *Sound: Dialogue, Music, and Effects*, ed. Kathryn Kalinak (New Brunswick, NJ: Rutgers University Press, 2015), 103.
40 Schweiger, "The Madman and His Muse," 26.
41 Hughes, *The Complete Lynch*, 41.
42 Woods, *Weirdsville USA*, 19.
43 Halsall, *The Films of David Lynch*.
44 Halsall, *The Films of David Lynch*.
45 Davison, "Demystified, Remystified, and Seduced by Sirens," 142.
46 Hainge, *Noise Matters*, 178.
47 Hainge, *Noise Matters*, 182.
48 Frances Morgan, "Darkness Audible: Sub-Bass, Tape Decay and Lynchian Noise," in *The End: An Electric Sheep Anthology*, ed. by Virginian Selavy (London: Strange Attraction Press, 2011), 189.
49 Liz Greene, "Interview 1: Sound Recording, Sound Design, and Collaboration—An Interview with Ann Kroeber," in *The Palgrave Handbook of Sound Design and Music*, eds. Liz Greene and Danijela Kulezic-Wilson (New York: Palgrave Macmillan, 2016), 37.
50 Olson, *David Lynch*, 129.
51 Van Elferen, "Dream Timbre," 185.
52 Van Elferen, "Dream Timbre," 186.
53 Morgan, "Darkness Audible," 190.
54 Ed Naha, *The Making of Dune* (New York: Berkeley Books, 1984), 229.
55 Gentry, "Alan Splet and Sound Effects for *Dune*," 70.
56 Wilson, "David Lynch's Metaphysical Sound Design," 123.
57 Wilson, "David Lynch's Metaphysical Sound Design," 123.
58 James D. Reid and Candace R. Craig, *Agency and Imagination in the Films of David Lynch: Philosophical Perspectives* (Lanham, MD: Lexington Books, 2019), 88.
59 Alexander, *The Films of David Lynch*, 21.
60 Tim Hewitt, "Is There Life After *Dune*? (1986)," in *David Lynch: Interviews*, ed. Richard A. Barney (Jackson: University Press of Mississippi, 2009), 29.
61 Chion, *David Lynch*, 76.
62 Gentry, "Alan Splet and Sound Effects for *Dune*," 68.

63 Gentry, “Alan Splet and Sound Effects for *Dune*,” 68.
64 Gentry, “Alan Splet and Sound Effects for *Dune*,” 64.
65 Gentry, “Alan Splet and Sound Effects for *Dune*,” 66.
66 Rogers, “The Audiovisual Eerie,” 247.
67 Greene, “From Noise,” 29.
68 Alexander, *The Films of David Lynch*, 119.
69 Davison, “‘Up in Flames,’” 127.
70 Chris Douridas, “Interview” (1997), in *David Lynch: Interviews*, ed. Richard A. Barney (Jackson: University Press of Mississippi, 2009), 158.
71 Eyes on Cinema, *Master of Sound: Alan Splet: Interviews with Peter Weir and David Lynch*, YouTube, 10:58, March 15, 2015, accessed January 12, 2019, https://www.youtube.com/watch?v=Y0-HCecz8FQ/.
72 *The Paris Review*, “David Lynch on Alan Splet,” YouTube, 12:57, May 13, 2014, accessed January 2, 2019, https://www.theparisreview.org/blog/2014/05/13/snapping-humming-buzzing-banging-remembering-alan-splet/.
73 Kenny, *Sound for Picture*, 129.
74 Davison, “Demystified, Remystified, and Seduced by Sirens,” 137.
75 Sanger, *Making the Elephant Man*, 118.
76 Davison, “Demystified, Remystified, and Seduced by Sirens,” 137.
77 Special to *Studio Daily*, “Sound Designer Randy Thom on a Career in Film Sound,” *Studio Daily*, January 24, 2014, accessed March 2, 2019, http://www.studiodaily.com/2014/01/sound-designer-randy-thom-on-a-career-in-film-sound/.
78 Colin Joyce, “This is Why the New ‘Twin Peaks’ Sounds as Weird as Shit,” *Noisey.com*, August 18, 2017, accessed October 9, 2018, https://noisey.vice.com/en_us/article/wjjxe9/this-is-why-the-new-twin-peaks-sounds-weird-as-shit/.
79 Chris O’ Falt, “Sound Comes First: Inside David Lynch’s Bunker, Where He Started Creating the ‘Twin Peaks’ Sound Design Over 7 Years Ago,” *IndieWire*, May 17, 2018, accessed October 2, 2018, https://www.indiewire.com/2018/05/twin-peaks-the-return-sound-design-david-lynch-hidden-studio-process-dean-hurley-1201965234/.
80 Tony McKibbin, “Listening to Lynch,” *Film Ireland* 115 (2007): 32.
81 Reid and Craig, *Agency and Imagination in the Films of David Lynch*, 172.
82 Patrizia Lombardo, *Memory and Imagination in Film: Scorsese, Lynch, Jarmusch, Van Sant* (New York: Palgrave Macmillan, 2014), 200.
83 Van Elferen, “Dream Timbre,” 179–80.
84 Andersen, “Behind the Weird Wonderful Sound of ‘Twin Peaks: The Return.’”
85 Sanger, *Making The Elephant Man*, 118.
86 Phone interview with Dean Hurley, May 21, 2021.
87 Andersen, “Behind the Weird Wonderful Sound of ‘Twin Peaks: The Return.’”
88 Andersen, “Behind the Weird Wonderful Sound of ‘Twin Peaks: The Return.’” Emphasis original.
89 Lynch refers to specific sound effects as hard effects in “Eyes on Cinema, *Master of Sound: Alan Splet*.”
90 Davison, “Demystified, Remystified, and Seduced by Sirens,” 135.
91 David Lynch, *Lost Highway*, script, June 21, 1995, accessed March 1, 2019, http://www.lynchnet.com/lh/lhscript.html.
92 Hughes, *The Complete Lynch*, 77.
93 Colin Odell and Michelle LeBlanc, *David Lynch* (Harpender: Kamera Books, 2007), 161.
94 “Love, Death, Elvis & Oz: The Making of ‘Wild at Heart,’” DVD, *Wild at Heart*, 2004.
95 Robert Robertson, *Cinema and the Audiovisual Imagination: Music, Image, Sound* (London and New York: I.B. Taurus, 2015), 26.

96 Andrea Virginás, "Television and Video Screens in Filmic Narratives: Medium Specificity, Noise, and Frame-Work," *Acta Universitatis Sapentiae, Film and Media Studies* 17 (2019): 93.
97 Odell and LeBlanc, *David Lynch*, 127.
98 Halskov, "'My Dog Barks Some'."
99 Lynch, *Lost Highway*.
100 Robertson, *Cinema and the Audiovisual Imagination*, 21.
101 Zeynep Toraman, "'What Is Gordon Cole Listening To?' The Rhetoric of Subjective Sound in *Twin Peaks: The Return*," in *The Music of Twin Peaks: Listen to the Sounds*, eds. Reba Wissner and Katherine Reed (Abingdon and New York: Routledge, 2021), 141.
102 Kyle Barrett, "Smashing the Small Screen: David Lynch, *Twin Peaks*, and Reinventing Television," in *Approaching Twin Peaks: Critical Essays on the Original Series*, eds. Eric Hoffman and Dominic Grace (Jefferson, NC: McFarland and Co., 2017), 57.
103 Barrett, "Smashing the Small Screen," 58.
104 Hurley quoted in O'Falt, "Sound Comes First."
105 O'Falt, "Sound Comes First."
106 Burt, "Is It the Wind," 261–2.
107 Jason Di Rosso, "Dean Hurley Is David Lynch's Long Time Sound and Music Collaborator," "The Screen Show," Australian Broadcasting Company, November 15, 2018, accessed February 15, 2019, https://abcmedia.akamaized.net/rn/podcast/2018/11/sch_20181115_1020.mp3.
108 Phone interview with Dean Hurley, May 21, 2021.
109 Kenny, *Sound for Picture*, 133.
110 Rodley, *Lynch on Lynch*, 242. Emphasis in original.
111 Andersen, "Behind the Weird, Wonderful Sound of 'Twin Peaks: The Return.'"
112 Phone interview with Marek Zebrowski, February 26, 2021.
113 Sanger, *Making The Elephant Man*, 118.
114 Colin Marshall, "What David Lynch Can Do with a 100-Year-Old Camera and 52 Seconds of Film," *Open Culture*, May 9, 2012, accessed November 2, 2018, http://www.openculture.com/2012/05/what_david_lynch_can_do_with_a_100-year-old_camera_and_52_seconds_of_film.html/.
115 Noel Murray, "'I Love Winds': David Lynch on the Sound of 'Twin Peaks,'" *The New York Times*, August 17, 2017, accessed October 2, 2018, https://www.nytimes.com/2017/08/17/arts/television/david-lynch-twin-peaks-interview.html/.
116 Greene, "Interview 1," 38.
117 Elizabeth Alsop, "'It's No Longer Your Film': Fictions of Authorship in Lynch's *Mulholland Drive*," *Journal of Film and Video* 71, no. 3 (2019): 60.
118 McGill, "The Contemporary Hollywood Film Soundtrack," 174.
119 McGill, "The Contemporary Hollywood Film Soundtrack," 236.
120 Kenny, *Sound for Picture*, 133.
121 David Lynch, "Action and Reaction," April 17, 1998, in *Soundscape: The School of Sound Lectures*, 1998–2001, eds. Larry Sider, Diane Freeman, and Jerry Sider (London and New York: Wallflower Press, 2003), 49.
122 Andrew Hageman, "The Uncanny Ecology of *Mulholland Drive*," in *Back to Mulholland Drive: Minimal Fantasy*, ed. Nicolas Bourriaud (Milan: Silviana Editoriale, 2017), 153.
123 *The Paris Review*, "David Lynch on Alan Splet."
124 Michel Ciment and Hubert Niogret, "Interview with David Lynch" (1990) in *David Lynch: Interviews*, ed. Richard A. Barney (Jackson: University Press of Mississippi, 2009), 109.
125 Kaleta, *David Lynch*, 175.

126 Gentry, "Alan Splet and Sound Effects for *Dune*," 70.
127 "Interview with Alan Splet."
128 Shaun Farley, "Ann Kroeber Special: BBC Interview," *Designing Sound*, October 25, 2011, accessed February 28, 2011, http://designingsound.org/2011/10/25/ann-kroeber-special-bbc-interview/.
129 Gentry, "Alan Splet and Sound Effects for *Dune*," 66.
130 Gentry, "Alan Splet and Sound Effects for *Dune*," 64.
131 A FRAP (or Flat Response Audio Pickup) is a compact microphone that was developed by engineer Arnie Lazarus that could fit anywhere—Kroeber estimated that it was the size of her pinky finger. See Smith, "The Auteur Renaissance," 102–3.
132 Gentry, "Alan Splet and Sound Effects for *Dune*," 64.
133 Smith, "The Auteur Renaissance," 102–3.
134 Gentry, "Alan Splet and Sound Effects for *Dune*," 65–6.
135 McGowan, *The Impossible David Lynch*, 97.
136 Martha P. Nochimson, *David Lynch Swerves: Uncertainty from Lost Highway to Inland Empire* (Austin: University of Texas Press, 2014), 71–72.
137 Gentry, "Alan Splet and Sound Effects for *Dune*," 63.
138 Min Chen, "How *Twin Peaks* Got Its Super Creepy Sound," *Surface*, September 15, 2017, accessed September 28, 2018, https://www.surfacemag.com/articles/dean-hurley-on-twin-peaks-anthology-resource-vol-1/.
139 Chen, "How *Twin Peaks* Got Its Super Creepy Sound."
140 Greene, "Bringing Vinyl into The Digital Domain," 97.
141 Liz Greene, "The Labour of Breath: Performing and Designing Breath in Cinema," *Music, Sound, and the Moving Image* 10, no. 2 (2016): 116.
142 Smith, "The Auteur Renaissance," 103.
143 Hughes, *The Complete Lynch*, 231.
144 Hageman, "The Uncanny Ecology of *Mulholland Drive*," 151.
145 Davison, "'Up in Flames'," 128.
146 Davison, "'Up in Flames'," 128.
147 Robertson, *Cinema and the Audiovisual Imagination*, 18–19.
148 Schweiger, "The Madman and His Muse," 26.
149 Lynch, "Action and Reaction," 51.
150 Schweiger, "The Madman and His Muse," 26.
151 Jordan Ruimy, "David Lynch: 'If You're Playing a Movie on a Phone, You Will Never in a Trillion Years Experience the Film,'" *World of Reel*, December 30, 2019, https://www.worldofreel.com/blog/2019/12/flashback-david-lynch.
152 In a phone conversation with Dean Hurley on May 21, 2021, he mentioned that Lynch also did this for *Inland Empire*.
153 Phone interview with Dean Hurley, May 21, 2021.
154 Kaleta, *David Lynch*, 95–6.
155 David Lynch, *Blue Velvet*, undated script, accessed January 3, 2019, http://www.lynchnet.com/bv/bvscript.html.
156 Kingsley Marshall and Rupert Loydell, "'Listen to the Sounds': Sound and Storytelling in *Twin Peaks: The Return*," in *Critical Essays on Twin Peaks: The Return*, ed. Antonio Sanna (New York: Palgrave Macmillan, 2019), 272.
157 Murray, "'I Love Winds'."
158 Laura Macfehin, "Music Supervisor Dean Hurley Talks *Twin Peaks*," *UndertheRadar.com*, August 31, 2017, accessed February 9, 2019, https://www.undertheradar.co.nz/interview/913/Music-Supervisor-Dean-Hurley-Talks-Twin-Peaks.utr.

159 "Angelo Badalamenti on *Lost Highway*," in *Beyond the Beyond: Music from the Films of David Lynch*, eds. J. C. Gabel and Jessica Hundley (Los Angeles: Hat and Beard Press, 2016), 93.
160 Email correspondence with Angelo Badalamenti, September 24, 2021.
161 Lynch and McKenna, *Room to Dream*, 220.
162 Schweiger, "The Madman and His Muse."
163 Rogers, "The Audiovisual Eerie," 268.
164 Schweiger, "The Madman and His Muse," 26.
165 Wilson, "Neuracinema," 82.
166 Macfehin, "Music Supervisor Dean Hurley Talks *Twin Peaks*."
167 John Ross quoted in Kenny, *Sound for Picture*, 132–3.
168 Phone interview with Dean Hurley, May 21, 2021.
169 Gentry, "Alan Splet and Sound Effects for *Dune*," 64.
170 Phone interview with Dean Hurley, May 21, 2021.
171 Phone interview with Dean Hurley, May 21, 2021.
172 Dominic Power, "'This Is a Story That Happened Yesterday but I Know It's Tomorrow': David Lynch's *Inland Empire*," *The Soundtrack* 1, no. 1 (2007): 55.
173 Van Elferen, "'Dream Timbre,'" 180.
174 Davison, "'Up in Flames'," 129–30
175 Van Elferen, "Dream Timbre,'" 179.
176 McGill, "The Contemporary Hollywood Film Soundtrack," 226.
177 Rogers, "The Audiovisual Eerie," 256.
178 Woodward, "Snapping, Humming, Buzzing, Banging."
179 Morgan, "Darkness Audible," 202.
180 Di Rosso, "Dean Hurley is David Lynch's Long Time Sound and Music Collaborator."
181 Katherine Reed, "'We Cannot Content Ourselves with Remaining Spectators': Musical Performance, Audience Interaction, and Nostalgia in the Films of David Lynch," *Music and the Moving Image* 9, no. 1 (2016): 4.

3 Diegetic Music

David Lynch is a man who knows what he wants, especially when it comes to music and sound. Lynch does a lot of listening before deciding what kind of music his films need, even—and especially—before they are shot. He once recounted:

> I listened to tons of music and some of it talks to me for this scene or that. I don't really know why, but each piece that ends up in the film supports the scene and makes the whole greater than the sum of the parts.[1]

Therefore, Lynch's listening is part of his filmic and directorial process.

Lynch especially has intuition when it concerns pre-existing, or what Rodley calls "found," music.[2] In a recent *Masterclass*, he said that there may be ten pieces of music that fit a scene out of all of the music in the world, but only one will marry with it in a union; that is how you know it's "the right music."[3] It is no mystery that one of the most beloved and memorable aspects of Lynch's films—aside from their uncanniness—is the appearance of famous artists on screen. From Rebekah Del Rio in *Mulholland Drive* to [The] Nine Inch Nails in *The Return* (they are announced in the Roadhouse with the "the"), the appearance of these musicians within each film's diegesis helps to drive the plot and provide a link to our own world. But for all of the artists who appear in these films, either over the radio or in person, their sonic style in the films has one thing in common: they aurally channel the uncanny.

In this chapter, I will consider the sonic style of diegetic music in three parts. First, I will discuss the use of famous artists performing as part of the narrative. Second, I will discuss the diegetic music that is played on electronic apparatuses such as radios and Victrolas; for example, the car radio playing Roy Orbison's "In Dreams" in *Blue Velvet*—a scene so strange that Michael Atkinson contends that once seen, you can never listen to the song the same way again.[4] Finally, I will discuss the diegetic music that is sung or played by characters in the film, such as Dorothy Vallens's singing *Blue Velvet*'s eponymous song. Along the way, I will consider another important point in Lynch's use of pre-existing diegetic music: *how* he uses it.

DOI: 10.4324/9781003265450-3

Diegetic Music in the Script

As with his inclusion of sound effects in his scripts, Lynch also does the same with the diegetic music and, similarly, he does not indicate all intended music in a script. But descriptions of selected music in the script—sometimes with a specific title and sometimes with only a description—help us to understand the role that Lynch assigns to the music in the film. This is especially crucial when he intends to use a specific song in the script but must shift to another song for one reason or another. Sometimes, he expresses an idea for the music he wants to use. We can see his love and nostalgia for mid-century America in his films' music. In the script for *Blue Velvet*, for instance, he indicates that "sixties MUSIC plays, performed by a live band on stage."[5] Similarly, in *Wild at Heart* he writes that Lula "is listening to sad, nostalgic music."[6] These directions emphasize the importance of mood, time, and music in his films. Though the music may only trigger nostalgia in viewers who were old enough to remember the 1950s and 1960s, it could cause imagined nostalgia for those who were not old enough and think of those decades as a better time and place.

In the previous chapters, we have heard from people like Dean Hurley that deciphering what Lynch wants in his films for music and sound can be challenging, doubly so when working with a script. However, with the film at hand, we can see how this translation between film and script occurs. One of the oddest music descriptions in a Lynch film is in *Wild at Heart*, in which he specifies that the band, The Bleach Boys, "kick into some kind of Professor Longhair swamp mambo."[7] How did composer Angelo Badalamenti translate this into sound? The music comprises a 12-bar blues played by a small jazz combo consisting of trumpet, trombone, tenor saxophone, upright bass, and drums. It sounds more like a 1940s blues than mambo, so Badalamenti here took some liberties with Lynch's note in how he composed the piece.

In contrast with the above example, sometimes Lynch is oddly specific about the sounds he wants. In another example from *Wild at Heart*, as Lula has a flashback to her first abortion, Lynch writes: "ECU of pulsing vein in Lula's neck – LOUD VIOLENT HEARTBEAT SOUND – LIKE A DOUBLE-PEDALED KICK BASS DRUM."[8] These hyperreal sounds are indicated in the script very specifically because Lynch desires that they be executed exactly how they are described. For Lynch, these are important components of his story.

Like the hyper-specific instruction, the volume levels that Lynch desires appear often in the script directions, including fade-ins and fade-outs and directions about distance. In *Wild at Heart*, he describes the music in the speed metal club as "one hundred decibels of speed metal" followed by "suddenly everything is deathly quiet."[9] Thus, Lynch also represents contrasts of sound in the scripts. We find examples of this when he notes that there is suddenly silence or suddenly extreme loudness of music or environmental sounds.

But Lynch is nothing if not consistent. It is interesting to see the consistency with which he uses specific terms and directions in the music directions in his scripts. While Hurley noted that people think of the word "dark" in association with Lynch's works, there is some truth to that with how Lynch describes music in his scripts. For example, in *Blue Velvet*, Lynch asks for a "dark forest," with "the music becom[ing] fainter as we move suddenly under the grass."[10] So there is something to be said about Lynch's sonic style being dark. In an interview with Matthew Sweet for BBC3, Badalamenti said that Lynch brought out his dark side, but Lynch disagrees—he says that he brought out love from Badalamenti, that there's something in him that's beautiful and truthful, even if there is something dark.[11]

Americana

One musical style that can be firmly tied to Lynch is the Americana aesthetic,[12] and this is evident in both diegetic music and non-diegetic music. Norelli has defined the Lynchian Americana sound through Badalamenti's score for *Blue Velvet*: "As postmodern as it is melodic, Badalamenti had combined a pastiche of 1950s American pop music with the dark orchestral scoring of 1940s film noir."[13] Typically, in film noir scores of that era, ensembles were relatively small and the use of music was relatively sparse.[14] But film noir also had another distinct characteristic: defying the tonal quality of contemporary Hollywood film music, which Badalamenti sometimes does.[15] One aspect of Americana music concerns American popular music, especially from the 1950s and 1960s. The use of certain music from this era to firmly ground the audience in nostalgia occurred first in *Blue Velvet*, which Eugene Willet notes was used "to create and define his cinematic vision."[16] Thus, we can say that Lynch's future use of popular music, including rock and speed metal, as a crucial component of the filmic narrative can be traced as a through-line from *Blue Velvet.*

But it is not so much the use of these songs as how they are used that is consistent. We do not just hear the pervasive use of the same genres and music from the same eras; Lynch considers how the music functions along with the visual elements and the narrative. There is often a disconnect between what we see and what we hear, and this creates tension. For Lynch, there is an appeal in testing how far he can go in the use of this disconnect to create a psychological effect. One example is in *Blue Velvet*. Brian Walter points out that "Lynch's screenplay calls for 'very sweet music' over the much-discussed opening montage sequence," and this establishes a discomfort for the viewer through the use of contrasting visuals with a well-known mid-century popular song.[17]

Famous Musicians

One pervasive feature of Lynch's films is the use of musicians to perform within the film's diegesis. Typically, Lynch chooses musicians of two types:

non-mainstream musicians or musicians who are Top 40 artists, and usually there is no in-between in his choice.[18] We can see this in the case of the former with Nine Inch Nails (*The Return*) and the latter with Julee Cruise (*Fire Walk With Me*). In both cases, the aspect of performance is one of the things that make Lynch's incorporation of popular music fit into his sonic style. Among all of Lynch's works, none contains more live music than *The Return,* even if we forget about its 18-hour length. At the close of each part (with the exception of Part 8, in which the performance occurs at the episode's midpoint), a musician or band takes the stage in the Roadhouse (also known as the Bang Bang Bar) to perform what might seem like an unrelated number. These performers include those who have worked with Lynch on prior films, such as Rebekah Del Rio, Nine Inch Nails, and Julee Cruise, as well as artists who have never been involved with Lynch, such as Au Revoir Simone, Eddie Vedder, and Chromatics, and the material includes reprisals of songs from the first two seasons of *Twin Peaks*, such as "Just You" performed by James Marshall as James Hurley. Sometimes, for Lynch, it takes simply hearing a band to become enamored with them. As Dean Hurley has recounted, Lynch heard Au Revoir Simone and "fell in love with the quality of their voices, their songwriting" to the extent that "they became part of his sound."[19]

So, when it comes to popular music, especially in *The Return,* what is Lynch's sound? For the music of the Roadhouse, it is small ensembles, often guitar- and keyboard-based, with singers that typically have low voices, whether females or males. An unmistakable part of the Lynchian sound is the use of rock songs, specifically those from the 1950s and 1960s. The "covers" of these songs sometimes are happy accidents, such as Rebekah Del Rio's Spanish cover of Roy Orbison's "Crying" (1961) in *Mulholland Drive*, while others are intentional. Importantly, once Lynch finds a singer with whom he likes to work, he will include him or her in multiple films, just as he does with his actors and actresses. Sometimes this also applies to popular singers whose music he chooses to use, such as Roy Orbison. As Katherine Reed writes, "musical performance tends to be a tool by which [Lynch] draws the spectator into the plot, implicating us in its action."[20] This music brings us into Lynch's filmic world.

It would be remiss if one did not consider the plethora of performances that end each part of *The Return.* Lynch, as we know, is very deliberate in his choices for music and sound, and this is especially the case in *The Return.* While each musician appears in an episode that is starkly different from the ones before, there are moments when Lynch breaks with this pattern to offer moments of nostalgia from the original two seasons or even a bit of nostalgia from one of his earlier films (see, for example, the reprise of "Just You" and "Audrey's Dance," or the presence of Rebekah Del Rio at the close of one episode). A sample of a band's music can appear in episodes that, generally, are harsh and dark. What is remarkable is when a song does *not* fit the sonic style of the work as a whole. Such is the case with Lissie's "Wild

West"; upbeat and bright, the song sounds very much out of place given the other songs that are played in the Roadhouse. But Lynch makes very deliberate choices, especially when he chooses to deviate from his typical sound continuity.

Monique Rooney points out that the "'live' act[s] within the serialized drama becomes another element in the visually and aurally dense atmosphere rendered throughout."[21] This is most acute in the Club Silencio scene of *Mulholland Drive*. This scene contains multiple layers, beginning with the magician, Bondar (Richard Green), announcing "No hay banda! There is no band! Il n'est pas de orquestra! This is all … a tape recording. No hay banda! And yet we hear a band. […] It is an illusion." This informs both the audience and the characters Betty and Rita that what we hear is not what we think we hear. We see a trumpet player (Conte Candoli) who mimes playing over a recording, and the magician also conjures up the sound of a clarinet. We think this may be over once Rebekah Del Rio enters the stage, singing "Llorando," a cappella, Spanish language cover of Roy Orbison's "Crying." But we soon realize that her performance, too, was an illusion, as she passes out and is dragged offstage while a recording continues her singing. This is the second such scene in which pantomime and lip-synching is used in the film. The first is the audition scene in which we are deceived into thinking that the doo-wop music is being performed live.[22]

Car Radios and Victrolas

Anyone who is a Lynch fan knows that two of the most pervasive objects in the director's oeuvre are car radios and Victrolas—or just record players. Like other objects in the director's films, these objects and their corresponding sounds serve to center the audience and provide a real-world anchor and sense of fidelity through the sonic space, but sometimes they are amplified in interesting and fictitious ways.[23] One example is the loudly dubbed popping and hissing of Henry's gramophone in *Eraserhead* and the same kind of sound that emanates from Senorita Dido's phonograph in Part 8 of *The Return*. While we know that gramophones do make these noises, they are not as loud as Lynch dubs them in the film.

From the very opening of *Wild at Heart*, Lynch uses the music on the radio, Powermad's speed metal song "Slaughterhouse," to "deconstruct and reassembles rock 'n' roll, working backward through American music stylistically and geographically to country and blues, and ending at the metaphorical crossroads where rock confronts its roots as the so-called 'devil's music.'"[24] Sailor (Nicolas Cage) and Lula (Laura Dern) are clearly a part of the counterculture, as is speed metal music, and Lynch uses this genre to represent that aspect of their personalities. Thus, Sailor and Lula find themselves in speed metal clubs, surrounded by persons of the same caliber.

Lynch often plays with the diegesis; that is, what may have been diegetic earlier in a film later is non-diegetic, and vice versa. This creates a sonic ambiguity in which the viewer cannot always tell whether something is non-diegetic or diegetic, exemplifying what Robynn Stilwell calls the "fantastical gap between diegetic and non-diegetic."[25] Part of the interest in Lynchian sound comes from this notion that not only can we not identify its source or its sound components but also that we wonder whether only we can hear it or if it is also heard by the characters on-screen. We find examples of this in many of Lynch's works.

Narrative Characters

Tangential characters in Lynch's films, ranging from The Lady in the Radiator in *Eraserhead* to Rebekah Del Rio as La Llorona (The Crying Woman) in *Mulholland Drive*, are known to sing. While these characters do not narrate in song, they do sing songs that form crucial components of the narrative. Of these characters, probably the oddest one in the Lynchian filmic world is The Lady in the Radiator in *Eraserhead*. We see her in the film as she sings "In Heaven," whose lyrics were written by David Lynch and are underscored by Peter Ivers's music; Ivers also sings on the track in the film.[26] The song's form is relatively simple, consisting of one verse repeated thrice. The first line of the verse repeats three times with a final culminating line:

> In heaven, everything is fine.
> In heaven, everything is fine.
> In heaven, everything is fine.
> You got your good things
> And I've got mine.

While "In Heaven" does not obviously operate like a blues, the lyrical and harmonic structures very much call to mind the organization of a blues where the first line repeats twice and then concludes with a different line. The melody also repeats in a way in which we expect, repeating the melody for the first three lines of text. The chord structure of this song reflects that of the text and consequently forms a sort of a loop, similar to the way that Lynch looped the siren in *Six Men Getting Sick*. Therefore, while not obviously a loop, it is constructed as one that is inaudible to the viewers.

"In Heaven" is stylistically adjacent to the other diegetic music in the film, that of Fats Waller's organ music played on the record player. The film features three Fats Waller organ pieces: "Lenox Avenue Blues" (1927), "Stompin' the Bug" (1927), and "Messin' Around with the Blues" (1927). For Waller, these are just three of many tracks that he recorded on a church pipe organ. Jazz played on a pipe organ is unusual, so Lynch's choice to use these recordings was grounded in a very specific choice to portray the weird and the uncanny. It provides an awkward sound, as the instrument lacks the capability to swing.[27] Despite Waller's attempt to remedy this, the music that emanates often sounds stiff. Chion describes the use of the organ to play jazz as a juxtaposition of the sacred and profane, two things that are often at odds in Lynch's work.[28] Phipps mentions the processed sound of these recordings, noting their mechanical sound.[29] Similarly, the music also psychologically distances the listener.[30]

Like the character of Henry, the diegetic music here is anchored in a specific time and place to sonically orient the viewer. While we can assume that the film takes place somewhere during the 1970s, the music tells us that we are in a much earlier time, one that is in line with the simplicity of the industrial and organic sounds and sets. Therefore, the use of anachronistic music provides us with a sense of temporal uneasiness—where, exactly, in time are we? Or, in the words of Agent Cooper in Part 18 of *The Return,* "What year is this?" This sense of being in two temporal spaces at once—between two worlds—is a hallmark of Lynch's works.

Another of Lynch's frequent devices in film is surrealism. On Lynch's 74th birthday in January 2020, he released a short film on Netflix called *What Would Jack Do?* The film is a murder interrogation of a Capuchin monkey named Jack Cruz (credited as played by himself but voiced by Lynch) by a detective (also Lynch). At the end of the film, Jack sings a love song called "True Love's Flame" to his beloved—a chicken named Toototabon (played by herself). In Brazilian Portuguese, "Tudo a bom" means "all is well."[31] So, this variation in spelling on the Portuguese phrase for the chicken's name, the black-and-white picture, the smoky set, and the song could be one way that the film hearkens back to the Lady in the Radiator's song in *Eraserhead,* where "everything is fine."

Diegetic Scoring

When working with Badalamenti, Lynch does not depart from his use of jazz; we can see this in both the first two seasons of *Twin Peaks* and in *The Return.* And jazz sets the stage for *Mulholland Drive*, with the opening cue, "Jitterbug." This piece clearly evokes Glenn Miller-style jazz, which was popular at the height of the jitterbug dance craze. Badalamenti intended to channel Miller's style for this cue, but, as Badalamenti said, "it isn't done like 'In the Mood,'" although Badalamenti states that they recorded it in "an abstract way."[32] This notion of a jitterbug dance contest at the beginning of the film, accompanying dancers in 1940s and 1950s attire, sonically displaces us, leading us to believe that the film is set earlier than it actually is. Displacement also occurs during the film's audition scene, first as Carol (Elizabeth Lackey) lip-synchs Connie Stevens's "Sixteen Reasons (Why I Love You)" (1960) and then as Camilla Rhodes (Melissa George) "sings" (she is lip-synching through a recording)

"I've Told Every Little Star." While "I've Told Every Little Star" was originally written in 1932 by Jerome Kern and Oscar Hammerstein for *Music in the Air*, it reached popularity with Linda Scott's cover in 1961, which this performance uses, and Rhodes even looks like Scott.

Jazz and rock have other connotations in Lynch's films, specifically in relation to sex and/or violence. We can see this in three of his films: *Fire Walk with Me, Wild at Heart,* and *Lost Highway.* In fact, Badalamenti was said to revisit the use of jazz from the *Twin Peaks* universe in *Lost Highway*'s score.[33] In these films, the music represents a seedy environment, usually a club, and either highlights or foreshadows an event that will change the course of the film stemming from sex and/or violence. Typically, in these types of scenes, the music becomes more jazz-infused, louder, and dubbed at the forefront of the mix, and has a heavier synth use.[34] Film music scholar Clare Nina Norelli calls this music "doom jazz." because it foreshadows some disaster.[35] For example, the jazz/rock hybrid that is played in the Pink Room in *Fire Walk with Me* illustrates Laura's promiscuity but also foreshadows her death from her participation in the seedy prostitution ring in which she works. But what Badalamenti calls "cool jazz" is found in scenes that feature young, self-assured males. He describes this kind of music as having "finger-popping, cocktail-lounge electric piano, pulsing bass, and lightly brushed percussion."[36] This description can be applied to most of the jazz works in Lynch's output, except for doom jazz.

Another scene with diegetic music in a Lynch work occurs in a restaurant environment. The cue "Heartbreaking" plays a pivotal role in *The Return*, when the old woman tells Cooper-as-Dougie, whom she calls "Mr. Jackpots," how giving her the money he won from the slot machine changed her life. In this solo piano work, we see an expansion of Lynch's sonic fingerprint in how he, Badalamenti, and Hurley handle the diegetic music in *The Return.* In the restaurant scene in Part 11, we hear Badalamenti's "Heartbreaking." According to Badalamenti, Lynch left him a voicemail asking for a piece reminiscent of Giacomo Puccini for an Italian restaurant scene that was "warm with nostalgia."[37] He stated in the voicemail that "I need some Italian restaurant music. Gimme three songs: one of them should be kinda peppy, one of them should be slow and sad and heartbreaking."[38] Unlike most of Badalamenti's music, which is written before shooting, in this case the shooting came first and the music later, based on Lynch's directions.[39] In the scene in which it is used, Agent Cooper, still treated as Dougie, sees and hears the pianist (Robert "Smokey" Miles) playing music and immediately reacts. Like "Laura Palmer's Theme," "Heartbreaking" repeatedly struggles to ascend and then rapidly falls.

While many of Badalamenti's characteristic motives, such as suspensions, do not appear in "Heartbreaking," we do get arpeggiated chords that help to achieve the rising then falling motive so pervasive in his music. This is an example of how Lynch and Badalamenti may not choose to exactly replicate a style of music based on formula but rather use a particular mood or aesthetic when creating it. This is akin to Lynch's description of moods; Badalamenti, therefore, composes in moods.

"Heartbreaking" clearly contrasts with all of the other instances of diegetic music in *The Return*, including the songs in the Roadhouse and the music that emanates from Senorita Dido's phonograph. This music, "Slow '30s Room," as Frank Lehman has discovered, comprises nine looping chords that undergo transpositions that come from the right-hand vamps of the "Big Band Beat" disc for the Optigan, a 1970s novelty instrument. The music, therefore, serves to both sonically orient and disorient the listener, as much of Lynch's music does, but especially in the cases of music that serves to represent a period or style.[40] This repetition can be found in other instances of diegetic music throughout all eighteen parts of *The Return* but never so obviously as here.

Rhythm

One thing that tends to be common in many of the diegetic songs in Lynch's catalogue is the repetitive, steady, and driving rhythms that pervade the score. These rhythms are located in specific places, often containing music that is used to channel his Americana and nostalgia themes. This may be one reason why Lynch chooses to incorporate them into his films. But while not all of the diegetic music is rhythmically driving, the music that is appears at similar kinds of moments. For example, we hear this in Powermad's "Slaughterhouse" in *Lost Highway* as much as we do in Part 8 of *The Return* when we hear the music emanating from Senorita Dido's phonograph.[41]

Conclusion

In Lynch's films, diegetic music is one of the most crucial components, chosen by the director carefully, sometimes with the film being created around a song, as we have seen with *Blue Velvet*. In each of his films, we can get a sense of the director's preferred aesthetic. First, he gravitates toward music that can be defined as Americana and which channels nostalgia—either for him or which he feels will trigger nostalgia in the general viewer, whether that means 1940s big band jazz or 1950s and 1960s popular music. He also tends to use music with intense, driving rhythms found in jazz, hard rock, and speed metal. But he also includes current music from the lighter side, such as that by contemporary singer-songwriters. Diegetic music is not used to create ambience but it is nevertheless crucial to the storyline, even if this is not obvious. Lynch's use of music is crucial to the story but not always obviously connected to it, as I discuss in the next chapter, on non-diegetic music.

Notes

1 Mike Hartmann, "Lost in Darkness and Confusion," *The City of Absurdity: The Mysterious World of David Lynch*, accessed June 7, 2021, http://www.thecityofabsurdity.com/.
2 Rodley, *Lynch on Lynch*, 125.
3 David Lynch Teaches Creativity and Film, "Sound Design and Scoring."
4 Michael Atkinson, *Blue Velvet (BFI Film Classics)* (London: British Film Institute, 1997), 61.
5 David Lynch, *Blue Velvet*, screenplay.
6 David Lynch, *Wild at Heart*, screenplay.
7 Lynch, *Wild at Heart*, Screenplay.
8 Lynch, *Wild at Heart*, screenplay.
9 Lynch, *Wild at Heart*, screenplay.
10 Lynch, *Blue Velvet*, screenplay.
11 BBC3, *Sound of Cinema: David Lynch* (May 27, 2023), https://www.bbc.co.uk/sounds/play/m001m569.
12 William Weston Bennett, "Americana on the Internet: Listening to *Twin Peaks*," in *The Music of Twin Peaks: Listen to the Sounds*, eds. Reba Wissner and Katherine Reed (Abingdon and New York: Routledge, 2021), 173.
13 Norelli, "Suburban Dread," 39.
14 Richard R. Ness, "A Lotta Night Music: The Sound of *Film Noir*," *Cinema Journal* 47, no. 2 (2008): 54.
15 Ness, "A Lotta Night Music," 52.
16 Eugene Kenneth Willet, "Music as *Sinthome*: Joy Riding with Lacan, Lynch, and Beethoven Beyond Postmodernism" (Ph.D. dissertation, University of Texas at Austin, 2007), 70.
17 Brian Walter, "Wild Things: Music and Masculinity in *Something Wild* and *Blue Velvet*," *Music, Sound and the Moving Image* 6, no. 2 (2012): 176.
18 Martha Schulenberg, "The Music Is Not What It Seems: An Examination of Labor and Capital in the Music of *Twin Peaks: The Return* Series," in *The Music of Twin Peaks: Listen to the Sounds*, eds. Reba Wissner and Katherine Reed (Abingdon and New York: Routledge, 2021), 80.
19 KEXP, "How David Lynch Fell in Love with Au Revoir Simone," *KEXP Soundcloud*, 2018, https://soundcloud.com/kexp/how-david-lynch-fell-in-love.
20 Katherine Reed, "The Bang Bang Bar, Silencio, and Lynch's Audiences: Meaning and Musical Performances in *Twin Peaks: The Return*," in *The Music of Twin Peaks: Listen to the Sounds*, eds. Reba Wissner and Katherine Reed (Abingdon and New York: Routledge, 2021), 63.
21 Monique Rooney, "Air-Object: On Air Media and David Lynch's 'Gotta Light?' (*Twin Peaks: The Return*, 2017)," *New Review of Film and Television Studies* 16, no. 2 (2018): 131.
22 George Toles, *Curtains of Light: Theatrical Space in Film* (Albany: SUNY Press, 2021), 178.
23 Rogers, "The Audiovisual Eerie," 257.
24 Mike Miley, "David Lynch at the Crossroads: Deconstructing Rock, Reconstructing *Wild at Heart*," *Music and the Moving Image* 7, no. 3 (2014): 42.
25 Robynn J. Stilwell, "The Fantastical Gap between Diegetic and Nondiegetic," in *Beyond the Soundtrack: Representing Music in Cinema*, eds. Daniel Goldmark, Lawrence Kramer, and Richard Leppert (Berkeley and Los Angeles: University of California Press, 2007), 186.
26 Josh Frank, *In Heaven Everything is Fine: The Unsolved Life of Peter Ivers and the Lost History of New Wave Theatre* (New York: Free Press, 2008), 134.

27 Paul S. Machlin, *Stride: The Music of Fats Waller* (London: MacMillan Press, 1985), 44.
28 Chion, *David Lynch*, 43.
29 Phipps, "Industrial Soundscapes," 86.
30 Mark Mazullo, "Remembering Pop: David Lynch and the Sound of the '60s," *American Music* 23, no. 4 (2005): 494.
31 I am grateful to Patricia Weitzel for translating this for me.
32 Schweiger, "The Madman and His Muse," 27.
33 Norelli, "Suburban Dread," 41.
34 Burt, "'The Thread Will Be Torn'," 107.
35 Clare Nina Norelli, *Soundtrack from Twin Peaks* (New York: Bloomsbury, 2017), 118.
36 Ron Givens, "Creative Contrasts: Making Moody Music," *Entertainment Weekly*, April 6, 1990, http://www.ew.com/ew/article/0,,317090,00.html.
37 Daniel Dylan Wray, "The Secrets Behind the Music of 'Twin Peaks: The Return,'" *Pitchfork*, September 4, 2017, https://pitchfork.com/features/article/the-secrets-behind-the-music-of-twin-peaks-the-return/.
38 KEXP, "Twin Peaks: Who Signs that Cool Version of Viva Las Vegas?" July 24, 2017, https://soundcloud.com/kexp/twin-peaks-who-signs-that-cool-version-of-viva-las-vegas.
39 KEXP, "Twin Peaks: Who Signs that Cool Version of Viva Las Vegas?"
40 Frank Lehman, "Optigan Illusions: Sonic Dislocation in *The Return*," *Musicology Now*, December 20, 2017, https://musicologynow.org/optigan-allusions-sonic-dislocation-in-the-return/.
41 Reid and Craig, *Agency and Imagination in the Films of David Lynch*, 149, 238.

4 Non-diegetic Music

As I have so far established, Lynch's sonic fingerprint is recognizable almost immediately, creating a sound that, as Holly Rogers writes, "forges a distinctive sensory continuity within and between his works."[1] The ambiguity and interplay between diegetic and non-diegetic music is common in Lynch's films; this is most obvious in the first season of *Twin Peaks.* As Ron Rodman writes, in *Twin Peaks*, composer Angelo Badalamenti's cues follow Kevin Donnelly's concept of "music blocks," where very few cues are used to score the episodes and function as leitmotifs.[2] They can function easily this way, Rodman notes, because of how Badalamenti composed them, the majority of cues containing "elements of minimalism, with repetitious chord progressions, slow, meandering melodic gestures, and nonconclusive cadences."[3] Mark Frost confirms this use of music blocks when he discusses the music of *Twin Peaks*, referring to Badalamenti's cues as part of a sound bank for the pilot.[4] Lynch uses non-diegetic music to disquiet, disturb, and disorient the viewer in a sonically cohesive way that itself can be easily destabilized.[5] Session guitarist Ira Siegel remarked that at a recording session for one of Lynch's films (he could not remember which), Lynch and Badalamenti said that they thought that the odder the music was, the better.[6]

As previously I discussed, before collaborating with Badalamenti, Lynch worked with composers such as John Morris and the bands Toto and Nine Inch Nails. Some of what makes Lynch's sonic style consistent derives from his collaborations with the same people. One of these is driving rhythms, which are heard in all of his films. This is clear in the "Desert Theme" for *Dune* that Toto composed. In this chapter, I will focus on the sonic profile of Lynch's non-diegetic films and how it contributes to the narrative of the film.

Angelo Badalamenti and the Compositional Process

Angelo Badalamenti remarked on his working relationship with Lynch and how that affects his compositional process. Lynch typically sat down next to Badalamenti on his piano bench and described things as the composer played; Badalamenti "plays his words," according to Lynch.[7] As Lynch changes

DOI: 10.4324/9781003265450-4

what he says, Badalamenti changes what he plays until he gets what Lynch wants.[8] Given that the sonic profile for Lynch's films is so consistent, I asked Badalamenti if he thinks of his other scores when writing for Lynch. He replied, "I do not consider the music I've written. One request David always asks for me to compose is, "Angelo, write me your music, that's gonna tear the hearts out of people."[9] So, we can assume every score was a blank slate for Badalamenti.

Unlike most composers, who compose using the rough cut of the film, Badalamenti wrote the music during production, based on the general description of moods that Lynch provided. This stemmed from their working relationship. Badalamenti has said: "It's an incredible thing that we know each other so well that all David has to do is say very few words to me. He describes moods, and moods translate into music for me."[10] Badalamenti has also noted that he begins to compose his score before Lynch even begins shooting a film, and approached Lynch with ideas for the music. As Badalamenti put it: "He sees what he's going to shoot just by me playing this music."[11]

One of the core aspects of Lynch's sonic style is that it is mood-based, and thus there is a continuity of sound styles across his films. Badalamenti had a specific technique that he used to illicit sonic tension: "It is not the top melody or even the bass, it is something in the middle that kind of rubs wrong, and is maybe even mildly dissonant. You hear it, but it is not in your face."[12] He elaborated on the use of suspensions and harmonies in creating this sense of tension:

> There are two basic elements: melody and harmony. The melodies have a warm, simplistic feel, but then you take those melodies and you harmonize them in a certain way; I'm a sucker for suspensions. ... The harmonies I use are also dissonances that resolve, but sometimes as they resolve another dissonance comes up, and so you've got this weaving and overlapping that creates a beautiful tension.[13]

Suspensions are integral to the Lynchian sound. Badalamenti recounted: "David feels that music is the voice of his concepts. It's slow, moody, and menacing, with these beautifully dark suspensions that act as a middle voice that draws you into his stories."[14] But Badalamenti's music also features relative harmonic stasis.[15] Further, there are a few other things that are found across Badalamenti's scores for Lynch: "The amalgamation of styles such as jazz, American pop nostalgia and his own dark synthesizer-based sounds."[16] Sometimes Badalamenti's scores will defy any clear temporal association, as when, for example, they fuse 1950s pop with 1940s jazz.[17] For some films, such as *Inland Empire*, Lynch admits that Badalamenti's characteristic sound is easily heard; someone can hear it and know that he wrote it but does not elaborate any further on what exactly they are hearing or noticing.[18]

Thus, we can see that there are many consistencies in how Badalamenti composed for Lynch's films. As Isabella Van Elferen observes:

> Badalamenti's scores usually contain a small number of traditional elements, such as the occasional stinger for scare effects or leitmotifs tied to certain persons or situations. These well-known techniques are employed so unconventionally, however, that instead of being inattentively heard signifiers that pertain to on-screen events, as in traditional films, they draw attention to their own floating evasiveness. … Badalamenti creates moods of nostalgia for times that lie eternally locked in the past. Within this sentimental framework, the simultaneous presence of long, sustained synthesizer chords and endlessly looped, nonlinear drones provides continual warnings that tranquility can be deceptive. The ambiguity of Badalamenti's extra-diegetic music is increased by the ways it is used within the context of film narrative and visual imagery. By letting leitmotifs migrate among different characters and situations, by underscoring scenes with foreboding drones, and by avoiding an over-use of stinger effects, Badalamenti's scores for Lynch films undermine and gradually dismantle the unwritten rules of film-musical signification.[19]

Badalamenti's music for Lynch tends to lean on suspended and slow-moving harmonies, especially throughout *The Return.* We hear this most acutely in two of the more prominent cues: "The Chair"—used in two scenes—and "The Fireman"—used in one scene.

Even when Lynch does not know exactly what he wants for a film, he tends to gravitate toward certain sounds, including wind. When Badalamenti was instructed to compose a "Mysteries of Love" for *Blue Velvet*, he asked Lynch what he wanted. Lynch's reply was: "Oh, just make it like the wind or the ocean, let it float and put a little plastic in it."[20] When he began to think about the music for *Dune*, Badalamenti told Kenneth Godwin, he considered using orchestral arrangements of rock songs because he favors the sound of "massed Russian strings and choir to give it a soaring, ethereal quality."[21] In many cases, the sound of *Dune* departs from Lynch's typical style, and even in cues in *The Return*, such as "Accident" and "The Fireman," Badalamenti leans heavily on sustained shrieking strings whose sound aims to "unnerve and shock the audience."[22] Even when not using strings, Badalamenti writes slow-moving and sustained harmonies in the form of high-pitched tone clusters, such as those we hear at moments in "Audrey's Dance," which occurs in both the first two seasons of *Twin Peaks* and in *The Return.*

Main Title Music

Among the scores for Lynch's films, one of the first things that we notice is that there is a consistency in his main title music, regardless of whether the music was written by Badalamenti or another of Lynch's collaborators. The main titles for Lynch's films feature either a sense of darkness and foreboding or a dreamlike quality. We can hear the former quality, especially in the title music for *Mulholland Drive* and *Blue Velvet*. The latter is demonstrated through the prologue and main title of *Dune*.

The *Dune* prologue opens the film as Princess Irulan (Virginia Madsen) narrates what the viewer needs to know about the planet Arrakis and the spice. The opening of her narration is underscored with rapid descending harp arpeggiations, typically associated with virtuosity, followed by relatively static harmonies interspersed with short harp arpeggiations. This draws the viewer's attention to Princess Irulan's monologue more than to the music. The music is styled almost like a recitative accompaniment in opera. The prologue moves into the main title theme of the film, stopping on a tremolo that leads into repeated seconds over the melody that sound like tremolos. Tremolos, combined with minor keys in film, often indicate something sinister. As with Lynch's other collaborations with Badalamenti, he describes what he wants and Badalamenti plays on his keyboard until he finds what Lynch is looking for. This is a consistent process for the pair, as Lynch said that if you know what you want, you just have to bring it out of Badalamenti because it's already inside of him; he could do anything.[23]

We see some of these techniques in other works by Lynch. The main theme of *Mulholland Drive,* for example, like both "The Fireman" cue and "Laura Palmer's Theme" in *Twin Peaks*, has a slow, sequential rising and falling motion, suggesting that an attempt to reach a climax that is always thwarted. "Laura Palmer's Theme" is climbing and reaching for something. As Lynch put it, "Angelo goes to the stars and catches a thing and I'm there as his brother filling the air with freedom and energy to get it. It's so delicate."[24]

Orchestration

An often-overlooked element of Lynch's sonic style is the music's orchestrations. When Badalamenti composes, he does so on a synthesizer or keyboard, so it is not at all surprising that he incorporates the instrument into his cues. Further, he often combines the synthesizer with strings.[25] But he also tends to gravitate toward specific instruments such as guitar (typically electric), drum set, alto and tenor saxophone, and upright bass, instruments that are used frequently in both jazz and rock music. When we examine the music of Lynch's films, then, it is not at all surprising that many of the non-diegetic cues are in the style of one or both of these genres. As Kai West has demonstrated, the use of drums in Lynch's works is frequent.[26] Matthew Sweet remarks that having a slow purposeful drumbeat is characteristic of Badalamenti's music.[27] But it is not only drumming; it is specifically jazz drumming. We hear jazz drums throughout the *Twin Peaks* franchise, in the prequel film, in the original series, and in *The Return.*

For both Badalamenti and Lynch, orchestration is important, especially when an attempt is made to copy a sound. Badalamenti recounted that for *Blue Velvet* Lynch wanted him to write an arrangement of Bobby Vinton's song, "Blue Velvet," that would sound like the original 1950s record; he told Lynch that he would be able to do so by using some of the original instruments and emulating the original orchestration.[28] Another example is when Lynch asked Badalamenti to write a song that emulated the sound of This Mortal Coil's "Song to the Siren" (1983), also for *Blue Velvet.* What resulted was Julee Cruise's "Mysteries of Love." For "Mysteries of Love" Badalamenti replaced the guitar from "Song to the Siren" with synthesizer and added echo effects, but the aesthetic is the same.[29]

Orchestration and stylistic continuity in Lynch's films typically take two forms: within films and across films. Orchestration across films includes a reliance on the strings, saxophones, percussion, and the Fender Rhodes electric piano. Badalamenti did all the orchestrations for *Lost Highway*, which connected all the cues together by mood.[30] For *Mulholland Drive*, Badalamenti used an orchestra of sixty-two musicians, primarily strings, but with added synthesizer, brass, woodwind, and percussion mainly in the opening jitterbug and the magic scene.[31] Because of his work with Badalamenti, for many of his films, the orchestration remains relatively constant in all of Lynch's films, as he likes to use a similar palate for his works, often focusing on strings, brass, and synthesizer.

Both Lynch and Badalamenti are credited as composers on *Mulholland Drive*. He will tell Badalamenti to play Shostakovich and Wagner and somewhere in there he will play notes and then he finds them and elaborates on them, sometimes playing multiple things together—Lynch explains that they found things in the music together that resulted in the music for the film, especially the theme to *Mulholland Drive*, which is a combination of two of these musical "things" that they merged. In *Mulholland Drive*, the non-diegetic music is for the most part based on the main title theme. Badalamenti writes very similar slow harmonies for strings and synthesizer to "The Fireman" cue in *The Return*, and they are used again in *The Return*'s "Love Theme" cue. Music has to pass through the filmmaker so that it all holds together. Lynch says that he as the filmmaker makes the final decision on the music in the film as they translate to the screen.[32]

Pre-existing Music

Lynch famously selects the songs that will be used in his films before preproduction even begins.[33] When Lynch uses pre-existing pieces in his films as non-diegetic music, he uses them not only as narrative devices but also as disorienting devices. We can see this in *The Return* with two electronically manipulated pieces: Muddy Magnolias's "American Woman" (used in Parts 1 and 16) and Ludwig van Beethoven's *Moonlight Sonata* (used in Part 8), both of them slowed down to at least half speed. But Lynch does not always manipulate the pre-existing music, as we can also see in Part 8 when he uses Krzysztof Penderecki's *Threnody for the Victims of Hiroshima* (1960) in its entirety.[34] One effect that emerges from the slowing down of music such as "American Woman" and the *Moonlight Sonata* is that the sound becomes low and gives the illusion of dark, thick textures. A discussion of Penderecki's *Threnody* must also consider the director's love for the Polish avant-garde. Lynch's clear connection with the music of the Polish avant-garde, specifically that of Penderecki, is made clear in *Absurd Encounter with Fear* (1967), which features Penderecki's *Capriccio for Violin and Orchestra* (1967). Lynch also used Penderecki's *Polymorphia* (1962) and "Als Jakob Erwachte" ("The Dream of Jacob," 1976) in *Inland Empire.*

Pieces by Penderecki in the Cold War Polish avant-garde tradition create a visceral soundscape that attracted Lynch.[35] This is a style of music that Lynch would return to often. Composer Marek Zebrowski, with whom Lynch worked on *Inland Empire* and on his short film *Fire (Pożar),* recounted that he had Lynch and his wife, Emily Stofle, over to his house for dinner and Lynch asked him to play Polish avant-garde music.[36] Lynch gravitated toward that style, using it from his earliest short films through his most recent works.

Penderecki's *Threnody, Polymorphia,* and *Capriccio,* along with Zebrowski's *Fire* (*Pożar*), are representative of the Polish avant-garde style of which Lynch is so fond: they feature disorienting, constantly shifting textures that change from thick to thin and back again, and high string timbres, specifically those that use tremolos, harmonics, and *col legno* bowings. As used in Lynch's films, the *col legno* bowings and tremolos often play on the horror-film conventions in which these musical conventions are sometimes used.

Lynch also uses pre-existing Western art music as a disorienting device. An example is the use of Richard Strauss's "Im Abendrot" ("At Dusk") from his *Four Last Songs* (1948), used suddenly after speed metal to startle the viewer in *Wild at Heart.* In *The Elephant Man,* Lynch uses Samuel Barber's *Adagio for Strings* (1936) in the film's final scenes. He was specific in the version he used, that by Andr Previn, which he first heard on the radio and then confirmed after listening to nine other versions.[37] The Barber piece, like many pieces of pre-existing music and original cues, is based on a rising and falling pattern that suggests the music can never quite achieve an apex.

But Western art music and popular songs are not the only types of pre-existing music that Lynch uses in his films. Jazz is also used in a variety of ways, and often for comedic effect. In *The Return,* Dave Brubeck's "Take Five" is used to underscore Cooper-as-Dougie's addiction to coffee.[38] Cooper-as-Dougie is a bumbling, comical character who is trying to find his way in the world after being stuck in the Black Lodge for 25 years, so it only makes sense that his confusion about how to eat and drink is underscored by a syncopated piece in quintuple time. "Take Five" opens with a drum solo that establishes the meter, followed by a piano and bass guitar entrance that set up the syncopated manner of the piece. Finally, in measure 12, the alto saxophone enters on beat 4, a strong beat in quintuple meter. This disorients the listener because in common time, beat 4 is typically a weak beat. The emphasis results in an off-kilter feeling that reflects Dougie-as-Cooper's clumsiness and his attempt to be a normal human being in the real world.

The closing credits of *Inland Empire* combine Lynch's use of jazz and lip-synching, as one of the dancing women in the front lip-synchs Nina Simone's "Sinnerman" (1962). Simone's version of a traditional undated song by Will Holt opens with a syncopated, driving vamp. But there are other instances of pre-existing music. Hurley discussed this in the case of one scene in *The Return*:

> There's something there in terms of the evolution of historical working methods of scoring a film. Traditionally, he has his encounters with that. But it drifts away because his vision is so strong that he'd rather create music to be idea and then let it fall into place. Here's a good practical example on *The Return*: Richard Horne runs over the little boy and you've got that incredible Angelo piece of music that swells and does all this stuff. So, that's an example where that piece of music existed before principal photography. It was literally David describing the scene to Angelo and Angelo's playing. Now, when that scene is cut together, Duwayne Dunham, the editor, cuts largely without music and his philosophy is he's trying to find the internal abstract rhythm of the scene. He said, "When I do that, I find that music will just naturally fall into place, because there's a musicality to the cutting." And so, when that piece of Angelo's that David talked through the script to Angelo and Angelo played, that piece ended up in the scene. Duwayne had never even heard the music. And then that piece ends up getting laid in and it was almost like the whole thing was just meant to be. It's not like there was a lot of music editing or anything, it just lays in there. And it works and that's where it's the esoteric notion of it all, it's this fundamental note and his collaborators and practitioners become sympathetically vibrating with that fundamental note. Then it all comes together so effortlessly and easily, because there's this purity of the idea. It's crazy. That definitely was a wow moment. For me, we're just seeing that happen.[39]

This emphasizes that music is often composed before pre-production even begins.

David Lynch Theater and Lynch's Short Films

At the start of the COVID-19 pandemic in early 2020, David Lynch released several short films on his new David Lynch Theater YouTube channel.[40] Fans could now see, for the first time, many of his films that dated as far back as the 1960s. These short films can tell us a lot about how Lynch uses and has used non-diegetic underscoring and about how his sonic style has evolved, regardless of the composer with whom he worked.

Harkening back to Lynch's earliest short films, such as *Six Men Getting Sick*, *Fire* (*Pożar*) from 2015 is an animated surrealist film that lasts roughly ten minutes. The film illustrates the consequences of the lighting of a single match, causing every subsequent event to spiral out of control. Thus, the music of the film reflects the causation of the events that stem from one event.

Fire (*Pożar*) was a collaboration between Lynch and composer Marek Zebrowski. As mentioned earlier, Zebrowski worked with Lynch on *Inland Empire*, and the two often improvised together (see Figures 4.1 through 4.4 for photos of the two improvising). One occasion of their improvisation was as an introduction to the premiere of *Inland Empire* at the 2006 Camerimage Film Festival in Łódź. On this improvisation, Zebrowski recounted:

> David was really thrilled to do this concert since it was held on the main stage of Łódź Grand Theatre. As we were finishing our improvisation, David gave a very discrete signal to the stagehand, who began to gradually lower us into the orchestra pit. As we were gradually vanishing from view, the ominous music and opening credits of the film came up on screen. It was a great introduction of that film.[41]

Figure 4. 1 David Lynch and Marek Zebrowski Improvising at the Premiere of *Inland Empire* (Photo Credit: Camerimage Festival staff photographers. Photo courtesy of Marek Zebrowski)

Figure 4.2 David Lynch and Marek Zebrowski Improvising at the University of Southern California, March 2011 (Photo credit: Charles Bragg. Photo courtesy of Marek Zebrowski)

Improvisation is important to Lynch, and his work with Zebrowski is grounded in this practice.[42]

Zebrowski scored *Fire* (*Pożar*) for string quartet and the resulting work was meant to accompany the film; the stand-alone piece had its own name, *Music for David*, and the film's title was a surprise for Zebrowski.[43] Zebrowski recounted his process for writing the film's music, noting the importance of his and Lynch's improvisations:

> For David's project (like all other scoring jobs I did), I'm always guided by what's needed in a scene or a film rather than recycle some already existing templates. David and I have this long history of free keyboard improvisations; they certainly established a type of harmonic language that we've employed in our music-making in studio and in concert.[44]

Later, in a different communication, Zebrowski elaborated much more on this:

> David, when he finally called me, he said, "I have the film ready for your viewing." So, he invited me to this theater in his house, a small little screening room. And we sat there also with the animator Mariko [Miyakawa] and he just played it once. And then he looked at me and I said, "could we do

Figure 4.3 David Lynch and Marek Zebrowski Improvising in Paris at the Fondation Cartier, March 2007 (Photo Credit: Dean Hurley. Photo courtesy of Marek Zebrowski). Note: Zebrowski described this photo in the email in which he provided it to me on May 24, 2021: "We planned to have one performance only, but as there were literally thousands of people in the street waiting to get in, we played three sets and finished only around midnight. The crowds were still on the streets and very disappointed that the organizers announced the closing of the building for the night."

it again?" Because the film is running totally silent. But the minute I saw things, I started hearing music. So, when you ask me whether it's a visceral reaction, I think for me at least, it always is. We just react to visual stimuli the way the way he reaches to rip something in your soul or pluck some strings or whatever metaphor you want to use. It's just that first emotional connection to what you see. And then you try to recapture it by actually writing music, putting notes on the staff lines, and making sure that that you can recapture that feeling. It's almost like when you're dreaming and you want to remember your dream in the morning. It's such a difficult job to do that, right? So, it's the same thing. There is this kind of visual noise and then you see the proscenium of an old-fashioned theater. And I instantly heard this technique that is used on strings because I knew it would be a string quartet because we were collaborating with the Penderecki String Quartet who were going to perform the live accompaniment in concert;

Figure 4.4 David Lynch and Marek Zebrowski Improvising at the Polish Consulate in New York City, October 2006 (Photo Credit: Jerzy Kos. Photo courtesy of Marek Zebrowski)

it would be a premiere of both the video and the music, so I knew it was a string quartet. And there is a technique called *col legno*, which uses the wooden part of the of the bow on the strings. That creates this kind of a bony sound which are completely undetermined, but they make this kind of a noise. I just thought the title was David's surprise to me. But of course, it makes perfect sense. It goes back to the discovery of fire and everything else. But just a crackling sound. I tried to somehow recreate by using four string instruments. That's my visceral reaction for this particular idea. And I think it made sense to me at least and David seemed to have liked it when he finally heard that. We always trust each other in a sense. David and me, in the improvisations that we do, he just lets me go out and explore whatever is there to be explored right at the moment. And I think that's what characterizes almost everything that David did as a filmmaker. There was a sense of improvisation, immediacy, but the kind of exploring the unknown and not knowing what happens in the next second; that's the Lynch atmosphere that pervades every film of his and is hard to score. But you just have to trust your instinct that you also go into this dark room, you enter and you don't know what the layout is and whether you bump into any furniture or what.[45]

Like Badalamenti, Zebrowski does not consider Lynch's other works or even his typical sonic imprint when composing for his films. He stated: "I try not to be guided by it because it's very easy to sort of unconsciously, you know, just be influenced by some things. And it's always better to start with a tabula rasa, clean slate concept and see what speaks to you creatively and work it out."[46] The film guided Zebrowski's compositional approach and process, and the score sounds very much like the 'firewood' used in *Inland Empire*, which, coincidentally, Zebrowski worked on as a Polish translator. In composing the score for the short film about the consequences of fire, Zebrowski did not consider the musical "firewood" element that Lynch likes to use.[47]

Both Lynch and Zebrowski had things to say about the score for *Fire* during a talk at the University of Southern California. Zebrowski noted of his compositional process:

> I thought it was a very melancholic film in a certain sense and also very poetic. Without trying to be too explicit, I tried to illustrate further what David was doing. For example, there is something that looks like a hailstorm and I used a lot of pizzicato, but I also used a soaring melodic line to add a lyrical element to it.[48]

Zebrowski also was inspired by another scene in the film as he was writing the music:

> There is another segment towards the end of the film, which I call the Reindeer Ballet. When I saw that, I saw these intersecting animals floating through the frame; this is obviously a repeated a kind of a visual loop that that he used for this particular thing. I instantly thought of a nice little canon. And I came up with this Prokofiev-like dotted motif and I put it into a canon. Obviously, the listener or the viewer will not necessarily instantly grasp that technique but that is the connective tissue between the visual and the aural stuff. That's why I thought this is the way to score it. The way to score it is to, in some way, very gently and sort of in the background, refer to the technique. This was presented visually.[49]

Lynch considered the collaboration as an experiment, noting that "the whole point of our experiment was that I would say nothing about my intentions and Marek would interpret the visuals in his own way."[50] However, on reflection, Zebrowski stated:

> Once you let your child run free in the world, there's no way of stopping. David always says, "my films are out and people make all kinds of interpretations of them" and he never interferes. He never tells you what to see how what he meant because that's the beauty of it. There are 15

> different explanations for it. And I can tell you that, yes, pizzicato is there for the hailstorm. But the overall effect counts and it is it is a challenge just because this is a silent film with wall-to-wall music.[51]

Musical Vocabulary

Some of Badalamenti's themes are based on the same sorts of musical structures as in his other scores. In "Laura Palmer's Theme," for example, Badalamenti uses what Brad Osborn calls the subdominant tritone, or the "tritone that occurs above scale degree 4 in the bass," that occurs as emotional intensity heightens, typically in the context of an embellished fourth as an accented passing tone.[52] This theme can be divided into four parts:

> First comes a ponderous two-note pattern, the Dark Intro, which is an up-and-down drone that creates a tangible sense of doom. Next comes the Climb, a sudsy melody that parades up the scale oh-so-slowly, swelling with melodramatic fervor to the Climax. This orgy of feeling is the sort of thing that used to put viewers in the mood to watch *The Edge of Night*. Once this musical passion is spent, the melody begins to ebb, in what Badalamenti calls the Falling Part.[53]

One thing that becomes obvious is that drones, which I discussed in Chapter 2 as a component of sound design, are also important components in music. Examining both the harmonic vocabulary and the melodic movement of "Laura Palmer's Theme," we can apply this to other Badalamenti themes for Lynch to reveal a consistency in how he assembles his themes. Cat Hope reads Lynch's use of drones as "an allegory for the themes of urban dread and emotional flatness throughout his oeuvre."[54] When we examine his films and the use of drones, this seems likely.

Themes as Unifying Elements

In the context of *Twin Peaks*, Lynch excitedly told Badalamenti after he composed "Laura Palmer's Theme": "You just wrote 75 percent of the score. It's the mood of the whole piece. It is *Twin Peaks*."[55] This notion can be applied to Badalamenti's other film scores, as they typically gravitate toward one or more select themes upon which all others are built, whether melodically or harmonically. But Lynch also refers to other works when describing what he wants, solidifying the sense of sonic continuity. For example, according to Badalamenti, "David started out with *Twin Peaks* saying, 'This is *Blue Velvet* gone *Peyton Place*.'"[56]

For Lynch, music is half the picture and therefore it functions not as what Ben Winters calls "musical wallpaper," or non-narrative underscoring, but as a functional and unifying sonic object integral to the story.[57] But "musical wallpaper" also functions in other ways, such as continuous music that is found either as an addition to or replacement for dialogue. We can see the former in *The Elephant Man* where music is used in long stretches without dialogue and the latter in the first two seasons of *Twin Peaks*.[58] Badalamenti's themes often unify Lynch's stories, as in the case of "Laura Palmer's Theme" in the *Twin Peaks* universe.[59] As John Richardson has observed, "arguably all of the music in *Twin Peaks* is related in some way to the character of Laura Palmer," with cues "closely related thematically."[60] For instance, both "Audrey's Dance" and the "Twin Peaks Theme" are thematically connected.[61] It does not matter if the music is being used diegetically or non-diegetically—sometimes it is unclear as to which it is—but it is the music's presence that indicates what the audience should be paying attention to, and the musical unifying elements help to convey that information.

It is worth noting the coincidences that occur in Lynch's creative process. Before filming *The Return,* Lynch decided to re-record the themes from the first two seasons that would be used in *The Return* to make some slight alterations. As Hurley recounted:

> When they were recording the lower part for *The Return*, they wanted to play with some different variations, different instrumentation and stuff. They maybe [recorded] it five times in a row. I was taking these sessions because they were done remotely over the internet with Source Connect. I remember zooming out and seeing the MIDI information of "Laura Palmer's Theme" and being like, "Whoa, just looks like a mountain range": because it was. And then when I zoomed in, looking at a single instance of "Laura Palmer's Theme," I was just looking at twin peaks; it literally went up, down, up, down. We don't get this on staff paper because it's all broken out into measures but when you see a MIDI of a composition, the whole composition made the image of twin peaks, and I was just like that, in a nutshell, is what I'm talking about, the underlying theory or eerie and bizarre nature of an idea that has such a strong sense of DNA; it's sort of like how a leaf on a tree is made. It's all these complex veins, but nature's just somehow just sort of effortlessly manufactures this out. It looks complex, but there's like a unity to it all because of a singular genetic architecture or roadmap. It's the same thing with these ideas that David gets latched onto; they blossom out and everything somehow co-harmonizes because there's a similarity to everything and a reference point that he is constantly checking it, tweaking in order to know when these elements are right. But seeing that and showing it to David and sending it to Angelo, both of them were flabbergasted because it's just like, wow. David's response was, "it's cosmic!" But it's stuff like that where you're trying to desperately break things down into motifs, but it's like somebody was looking at the individual leaf on a tree and trying to take a little

> protractor and map out the distances between all the little leaf veins and everything, when you really need to go to underground to where the root structure of the tree is and look at that to figure out what's really going on. That's sort of the analogy because it's such a very unique thing that he does where the sum is greater than the parts. It's really, really wild.[62]

A few things emerge from this story. First, although it was unlikely that Lynch knew that the MIDI file of "Laura Palmer's Theme" would form twin peaks, especially since this is not visible in a musical score, the up-and-down motion is easily audible; this is another example of one of Lynch's "happy accidents." More crucially, Hurley noted in his account that there is a "similarity to everything" and this is reflected in the typical rising and falling motion that appears in many of the cues written by Badalamenti and other composers with whom Lynch worked. There is, as Hurley mentioned, a sort of DNA common to all of the music in Lynch's works, even with him tweaking things until he feels they are right. What makes Lynch feel that they are right is a combination of his intuition and the similarities between the music and sound of his other works.

But it is not just the creation of themes that is important to Lynch's films. Hurley also discussed how the themes operate and their relation to "firewood," specifically in *Twin Peaks* and *Mulholland Drive*:

> I just wonder if he's wanting to get back to building it in the editing room like what he did with Alan Splet and *Eraserhead*. He's got all these cues now with *Twin Peaks* that he can use like firewood. They're already there when they start editing and as the series went on, there was like this master set of data created with every single cue so every editor who came on board later, he's like, "here's the music library." I think there would be an occasion where Angelo would pop in because they needed something they didn't have. But I think what most people don't realize is *Twin Peaks*' score was not written as a picture. And then they continue that method of working a lot with the other films, famously with *Mulholland Drive* writing the theme. He's got the theme before principal photography and then going to Prague and doing this experimental approach. I think that's a very interesting thing that you don't see any other director doing quite like that.[63]

It is likely that Lynch drew on his typical sound, that which was created first in *Eraserhead* and then used in subsequent works. This would be consistent with his approach in *The Return*, which not only featured more ambient sound than music, unlike the first two seasons of the series where the reverse was true. But Lynch also used elements—visual and aural—from his earlier works, including *Eraserhead* and *Mulholland Drive*—in *The Return*.[64]

Conclusion

As I have discussed in this chapter, there tends to be a sonic distinctness in the non-diegetic music for Lynch's films, much of which derives from Lynch's collaborations with Badalamenti. The most striking characteristics of this music are sustained chords with slow-moving harmonies and shrieking sounds in the upper strings and suspensions. Many of Badalamenti's scores for Lynch have a characteristic rising and falling sequential movement. The orchestration and use of the music blocks are also a constant among Lynch's works that create a specific sonic profile that is recognizable to the viewer. In the next chapter, I will discuss another crucial aspect of Lynch's sonic style: his use of the voice.

Notes

1 Rogers, "The Audiovisual Eerie," 244.
2 Ron Rodman, *Tuning In: American Narrative Television Music* (Oxford and New York: Oxford University Press, 2010), 283. Donnelly coins the term "music blocks" in his 2005 book, *The Spectre of Sound: Music in Film and Television.*
3 Rodman, *Tuning In*, 284.
4 David Bushman, *Conversations with Mark Frost: Twin Peaks, Hill Street Blues, and the Education of a Writer* (Columbus, OH: Fayetteville Mafia Press, 2020), 164.
5 Rogers, "The Audiovisual Eerie," 241–2.
6 Ira Siegel, Keynote roundtable panelist, "Recording Session Musicians in New York City," Music and the Moving Image conference, New York University, May 28, 2021.
7 David Lynch Teaches Creativity and Film, "Sound Design and Scoring," *Masterclass*, May 2019, https://www.masterclass.com/classes/david-lynch-teaches-creativity-and-film/chapters/sound-design-and-scoring.
8 David Lynch Teaches Creativity and Film, "Sound Design and Scoring."
9 Email correspondence with Angelo Badalamenti, September 24, 2021.
10 TheJunkBucket, "*Mulholland Drive*: Behind the Scenes," YouTube, December 3, 2017, https://www.youtube.com/watch?v=Ik0vi0Qm5ts.
11 TheJunkBucket, "*Mulholland Drive*."
12 Badalamenti quote in Halsall, *The Films of David Lynch.*
13 Channel 4 Television London, "Angelo Badalamenti On His Career," *Channel 4 Television Online* (London), accessed June 7, 2021, http://www.channel4.com/film/reviews/feature.jsp?id=111752.
14 Badalamenti, quoted in Schweiger, "The Madman and His Muse," 26.
15 Rogers, "The Audiovisual Eerie," 266.
16 Norelli, "Suburban Dread," 42.
17 Rogers, "The Audiovisual Eerie," 266.
18 BBC3, *Sound of Cinema: David Lynch*, May 27, 2023, https://www.bbc.co.uk/sounds/play/m001m569.
19 Van Elferen, "Dream Timbre," 181.
20 Channel 4 Television London, "Angelo Badalamenti on His Career," *Channel 4 Television Online* (London), accessed June 7, 2021, http://www.channel4.com/film/reviews/feature.jsp?id=111752.

21 Badalamenti, quoted in Kenneth George Godwin, *Dune: The David Lynch Files: Volume 2* (Orlando: Bear Manor Media, 2020), 142.
22 Philip Hayward, "Introduction: Scoring the Edge," in *Terror Tracks: Music, Sound, and Horror Media*, ed. Philip Hayward (London and Oakville: Equinox Publishing, 2009), 10.
23 BBC3, *Sound of Cinema.*
24 BBC3, *Sound of Cinema.*
25 Cat Hope, "The Bottom End of Cinema: Low Frequency Effects in Soundtrack Composition," in *Sound Scripts: Proceedings of the 2007 Totally Huge New Music Festival*, Vol. 2, eds. Cat Hope and Jonathan W. Marshall (Sydney: Australian Music Centre, 2009), 77.
26 Kai West, "Listen to the Skins: Drumming and Time in *Twin Peaks*," in *The Music of Twin Peaks: Listen to the Sounds*, eds. Reba Wissner and Katherine Reed (Abingdon and New York: Routledge, 2021), 203–204.
27 BBC3, *Sound of Cinema.*
28 *Mysteries of Love: The Making of Blue Velvet*, Blue Velvet DVD, 2002.
29 Julee Cruise was a singer and actress who frequently appeared in Lynch's films. The song, "Mysteries of Love," was written for the film *Blue Velvet* and became the song that drew her into fame among Lynch fans.
30 BBC3, *Sound of Cinema.*
31 Schweiger, "The Madman and His Muse," 27.
32 BBC3, *Sound of Cinema.*
33 Kulezic-Wilson, *The Musicality of Narrative Film*, 32.
34 For more on this, see Reba Wissner, "Krzysztof Penderecki's *Threnody for the Victims of Hiroshima* and the Trinity Atomic Bomb Test in *Twin Peaks: The Return*," *Musicology Now*, December 21, 2017, http://www.musicologynow.org/2017/12/krzysztof-pendereckis-threnody-for.html.
35 Lisa Cooper Vest, *Awangarda: Tradition and Modernity in Postwar Polish Music* (Berkeley and Los Angeles: University of California Press, 2020), 1–2.
36 Phone interview, Marek Zebrowski, February 26, 2021.
37 David Lynch, *Catching the Big Fish: Meditation, Consciousness, and Creativity*, 10th Anniversary Edition (New York: TarcherPerigee, 2016), 43.
38 West, "Listen to the Skins," 213.
39 Phone interview with Dean Hurley, May 21, 2021.
40 David Lynch Theater, accessed September 14, 2020, https://www.youtube.com/c/DAVIDLYNCHTHEATER/videos.
41 Personal email communication with Marek Zebrowski, May 24, 2021.
42 Personal email communication with Marek Zebrowski, September 10, 2020.
43 Phone interview with Marek Zebrowski, February 26, 2021.
44 Personal email communication, Marek Zebrowski, September 10, 2020.
45 Phone interview with Marek Zebrowski, February 26, 2021.
46 Phone interview with Marek Zebrowski, February 26, 2021.
47 Personal email communication, Marek Zebrowski, September 10, 2020.
48 Julie Riggott, "New Music Shines in the Projector's Beam," *USC Thornton School of Music*, April 9, 2015, accessed September 14, 2020, https://music.usc.edu/new-music-shines-in-the-projectors-beam/.
49 Phone interview with Marek Zebrowski, February 26, 2021.
50 Riggott, "New Music Shines in the Projector's Beam."
51 Phone interview with Marek Zebrowski, February 26, 2021.
52 Brad Osborn, "The Subdominant Tritone in Film and Television Music," *Current Musicology* 107 (2020): 62–64.
53 Givens, "Creative Contrasts."

54 Cat Hope, "The Bottom End of Cinema: Low Frequency Effects in Soundtrack Composition," in *Sound Scripts: Proceedings of the 2007 Totally Huge New Music Festival*, Vol. 2, eds. Cat Hope and Jonathan W. Marshall (Perth: Australian Music Centre, 2009), 77.

55 Givens, "Creative Contrasts."

56 Badalamenti, quoted in Givens, "Creative Contrasts."

57 See Ben Winters, "Musical Wallpaper? Towards an Appreciation of Non-Narrating Music in Film," *Music, Sound, and the Moving Image* 6, no. 1 (2012): 39–54.

58 For more on the use of musical wallpaper in *Twin Peaks*, see Reba Wissner, "Isn't It too Dreamy? Music and Nostalgia in *The Return*," *25 Years Later Site*, December 10, 2017, https://25yearslatersite.com/2017/12/10/isnt-it-too-dreamy-music-and-nostalgia-in-the-return/.

59 Michel Chion, *David Lynch*, 2nd edition, trans. Robert Julian (London: British Film Institute, 2006), 110.

60 John Richardson, "Laura and Twin Peaks: Postmodern Parody and the Musical Reconstruction of the Absent Femme Fatale," in *The Cinema of David Lynch: American Dreams, Nightmare Visions*, eds. Erica Sheen and Annette Davison (London: Wallflower Press, 2004), 82–83.

61 Andrew S. Kohler, "'Like Some Haunting Melody': The Laura Palmer Theme in the World of *Twin* Peaks," in *The Music of Twin Peaks: Listen to the Sounds*, eds. Reba Wissner and Katherine Reed (Abingdon and New York: Routledge, 2021), 190.

62 Phone interview with Dean Hurley, May 21, 2021.

63 Phone interview with Dean Hurley, May 21, 2021.

64 For examples of these "Easter eggs," see Joanna Robinson, "*Twin Peaks:* 20 Easter Eggs, References, and Callbacks You Might Have Missed," *Vanity Fair*, May 23, 2017, https://www.vanityfair.com/hollywood/2017/05/twin-peaks-season-1-easter-eggs-episode-1-2-3-4.

5 Voice

From backwards talking to sound manipulation through telephones, records, and recording devices, the human voice plays an important role in Lynch's films, so much that we can consider its use to be "the strongest aural element."[1] In discussing Lynch's sonic continuity, Holly Rogers cites "heightened room tone [and] drone-based synths" as partially responsible, but she also notes the important role of "ethereal female voices [and] reimagined 1950s songs."[2] Along with sound design and music, Lynch uses the voice—both speaking and singing—in very specific ways, destabilizing our expectations not just with *what* is being said but also *how* it is being said, and often the voice sounds different from what we expect. For instance, as a film progresses, the sound of a character's voice might change in order to serve the narrative or be imbued with effects that make the voice sound not human at all. How the voice accomplishes these narrative changes is the basis of this chapter. In this chapter, I consider how Lynch uses the voice for dramatic impact through its various modifications in both his feature films and his short films.

Sound Effects and the Voice

Lynch plays with the use of voice in such a way that it sometimes functions as an abstract sound effect. We have seen this in *The Grandmother* when Mark's parents unsuccessfully attempt to utter the boy's name but produce monkey sounds. Animal sounds are often used in Lynch's films to illustrate a character's predatory nature—obvious or hidden—or primal urges.[3] We can see this in *Wild at Heart* when the old man (Freddie Jones) comes up to Sailor and Lula in The Hurricane and quacks like a duck before he says anything, proceeding to speak nonsense while sounding as though he has inhaled helium. In *Blue Velvet*, Splet augments animal sounds that are used in the lovemaking scenes between Jeffrey and Dorothy.[4]

These effects given to the voice are done through pitch alteration. Dean Hurley remarked on how Lynch alters the pitches of voices in his films to achieve a specific effect:

DOI: 10.4324/9781003265450-5

> He's oftentimes thinking of Freddie Jones in *Wild at Heart* where you pitch him up, or Evil Cooper in *The Return* where he's slightly pitched down. Some of those interrogation scenes become elements of how you take a scene and tweak it a little bit more. Whereas most people wouldn't think of those elements as tweakable, he's able to take those and kind of skew them off to get at something that he's after.[5]

Lynch thinks of the voice as an alterable medium with which to uniquely enhance the sonic portion of the narrative and uses his previous films as a guide.

Voice in Script

As we have seen, Lynch includes directions on sound and diegetic music in his scripts, and these include indications of what to do with the voice. Often, these indications call for screams and laughter, many of which are described as blood-curdling, violent, wild, and crazy, and sometimes an instruction will combine two or more such indications. Looking to the film can help us understand how this is conveyed sonically and how it contributes to a sonic style for the voice. Screams are indicated the most in Lynch's scripts and, as we will see in the next section, they appear in almost every one of his films.

Sadly, all copies of the script for *The Return* were shredded after filming as per Lynch's directives.[6] However, some pages have surfaced in photographs, and this is important for how we interpret, for example, what was intended for the Woodsman in Part 8. The script indicates that when the Woodsman enters the radio station and takes hold of the microphone "the figure speaks disturbing, atonal, word-like mechanical sounds into the mic, going out over the air in a strange monotone."[7] This direction is simultaneously vague and specific and is an example of a situation in which Lynch will guide the actor during filming as to just how he wants the voice to work.

The Speaking Voice

Recording and processing styles have an effect on the speaking voices that we hear in Lynch's films. One thing that is often overlooked is that Lynch tends to gravitate toward the same handful of actors in his films, which also contributes to the effect of voice in his films. The voice plays an important role in *The Elephant Man*, where it serves as a way for Merrick to express his autonomy and humanity against a backdrop of animal and industrial sounds; for this reason, we can consider it the most important sound in the film.[8] The voice of Merrick's mother (Phoebe Nicholls) is heavily processed[9]; in *Inland Empire*, the technique used to record the voice of Nikki Grace/Laura Blue (Laura Dern) is different from that of the other characters.[10]

There is a strong preference for certain types of speaking voices. For instance, many characters in Lynch's works present with "low-volume, high-pitched voices with a lot of false air and little breath support."[11] Repetition of phrases, sometimes mechanically, is one way in which Lynch uses the voice to elicit discomfort. An example of this is the teddy bear of Johnny Horne (Robert Bauer) in *The Return*, which repeats "Hello Johnny, how are you today?" on a loop.

Mechanical mediation of the voice is frequent. Two examples of this are in *Inland Empire* and *Lost Highway*, where the voices are filtered through mechanical means or are heavily distorted such that they are uncomfortable to hear. For films like *Inland Empire* and *Lost Highway*, which can be considered horror films, it is the sound, especially that of the voice, that creates the sense of fear and tension that the audience experiences more than the visuals.[12] This mechanical manipulation of the voice appears at various points throughout *The Return*, but the most obvious example is that of the Woodsman and the Evolution of the Arm.[13]

Screams

Throughout Lynch's oeuvre, screams have appeared countless times. Typically it is a woman screaming, though not always. Sometimes, screams form a fundamental sound throughout a body of work and, as Ariana DiValentino contends, they are so important in the three seasons of *Twin Peaks* that Lynch specifically chose to end *The Return* with Laura Palmer screaming.[14] For Laura Palmer (and, at the end of *The Return*, Carrie Page), screams are used as a communicative device, something that also occurs in other Lynch works. Here, however, it is a communicative device of strong proportions.[15] Screaming, as Monique Rooney points out, represents a sort of "primal vocality (of breath and voice)" in Lynch's works.[16] In film generally, screams almost always indicate fear and violence, and are often paired with ambient sound or music, and Lynch's films are no exception.[17] It is worth noting that not every scream functions this way; one example of when it does not is the childbirth scene in *The Elephant Man*. Women are not the only ones who scream in Lynch films; occasionally, boys and men also scream, for very specific purposes. As I indicated in Chapter 1, Mark in *The Grandmother* screams. The end of *Lost Highway* features a scream that takes us into the film's credits.

Talking Backwards

As Kyle Barrett writes, the sonic marker in *Twin Peaks*' Black Lodge/Red Room is exemplified by the backwards-talking in the dialogue.[18] To produce the sound of the backwards talking, double processing was used: the actors spoke their lines backwards, and that recording was then re-recorded and played backwards.[19] This speech deformation is just another way that Lynch aurally represents the kinds of mutilation and manipulation that occur in his films.[20] This double processing, as Michael Goddard writes, subjects the speech to "demonic reversal."[21] The backwards-talking and manipulation of the voice in Lynch's works represent portals to other places; in the context of *Twin Peaks*, it is the portal to the Black Lodge.

Acousmatic Voices and Voiceovers

As Michel Chion defines it, the acousmatic voice is a disembodied voice that can be heard but its source is unseen. The disembodied voice, throughout Lynch's works, tends to be ascribed a certain power, whether that of control or that of disorientation. Lynch is pretty consistent with how he handles the acousmatic voice, and acousmatic sound, especially the acousmatic voice, is one of the most pervasive sonic traits in his films.[22] Among Lynch's works, *Dune* is the film with the most use of voiceovers and acousmatic voices, and it established how the director would use the voice in this manner in subsequent films. This represents what Amy McGill calls the verbocentrism of Lynch's films: Lynch "uses dialogue to effectuate a high level of exposition and communicativeness, which is typical of classical narration."[23] The use of the voice in this way helps to ground the viewer in understanding a film that may not have an obvious plot or may be set in such an otherworldly location that it seems beyond understanding. The voice, therefore, is used as an orienting device.

In Lynch's films that feature acousmatic voices or voiceovers, the voice plays a role of its own beyond that of the character from whom it is meant to emanate. This is obvious throughout *Inland Empire*, but especially at the beginning where the acousmatic voice serves to orient the viewer.[24] Much of this is because of the placement of the voiceover in the mix, for it is foregrounded over any other noise or sound.[25] Thus it functions in the same way as standard filmic dialogue that is meant to be heard as crucial to the film.

Acousmatic sounds, especially the acousmatic voice, take on a slightly different definition in the Club Silencio scene in *Mulholland Drive*. What we do not realize until the end of the scene is that Rebekah Del Rio is lip-synching, creating a sort of disembodied voice that is not obvious until she passes out. This is an example of a frequent Lynchian trope: he establishes where a sound is emanating from only to upend the audience's expectations. We also see this in the doo-wop audition scene that is being lip-synched. As David Laderman writes, "a voice that belongs to a body becomes acousmatic by virtue of the performance and recording technology within the narrative."[26] In this case, however, we are not sure whether the character is, in fact, lip-synching or if it is some sort of acousmatic effect in the same vein as the notion that we hear a band but there is no band or, in the case of the audition scene, if it is live singing or if the voice is coming from a recording. We do know that Lynch is using music to play with time: the voice we hear is from the past (as it is recorded) but appears to be from the present.[27] This is not simply a case of using the acousmatic, but it is an instance where Lynch deliberately separates the voice from the body in a way that they seem completely fractured.[28] This instance is one of several cases throughout his films in which the director combines "mime, music, and song."[29] This combination blurs both audience expectations and audience reception.

Where the lip-synching and, by extension, voiceovers, are placed in the mix is just as crucial as what they say. Typically, we find them in the foreground of the films' sound mix. In *Dune* and *The Amputee*, for example, Lynch foregrounds the voiceovers so that they become a focus.[30] But it is just as important to note when voices are not placed at the forefront, since this is what Lynch does most often. This backgrounding of voiceovers creates a deliberately mysterious environment.

The Singing Voice

In Chapters 3 and 4, I discussed the use of diegetic and non-diegetic music in Lynch's films, but I did not consider the role of the singing voice. The singing voice plays an important narrative role in Lynch's films. As Brooke McCorkle Okazaki writes, "songs, because of their fusion of music with human voice, possess a certain semiotic power," and when they are diegetic, they "dissolve the soundtrack's boundaries; they blur music, sound effect, and voice into a single aural object."[31] Films such as *Mulholland Drive* and *Blue Velvet* are grounded in narratives that surround music, and it is important to consider the role of the singing voice and any timbral consistencies that Lynch uses. One term that comes to mind when discussing the singing voice timbre in Lynch's films is "sultry." We hear this especially clearly in *Blue Velvet* when Dorothy Vallens sings the title song, when Julee Cruise performs of "Mysteries of Love" in the same film, and when Sailor sings "Love Me Tender" to Lula at the end of *Wild at Heart.*

Sultry can also be used to describe Rebekah Del Rio's voice in *Mulholland Drive* as she sings "Llorando." One important component of this cover is that it is a cappella, focusing the aural primacy on the voice rather than any external elements such as accompanying instruments. The key in which Del Rio sings, too, has implications for the sultry sound and the focus on the voice. As Katherine Reed observes, Del Rio sings in Orbison's original key; the beginning is in what Reed calls a "male-coded range" appropriate for a male singing and the ending is in a feminine-like range. In Del Rio's performance, this order is reversed, and we only hear a vocal range appropriate to the singer's gender at the end of the song.[32] As the song progresses, the volume and vocal expression increases, further drawing us into the sound.[33]

But aside from sultry, there is a tradition of the sad, betrayed, brokenhearted female singer in Lynch's films. Del Rio is a part of this, and she is joined by Dorothy Vallens in *Blue Velvet,* the Lady in the Radiator in *Eraserhead*, and Julee Cruise in both *Twin Peaks* and *Blue Velvet.* In each of these cases, the singing voices portray "unbearable feeling, unconscious trauma, intuitive meaning" that reflects "desire, sorrow, or loss; in each case, too, it is not only the song that is sung and its manner of performance but also the singer's vocal quality, typically a low alto with grittiness."[34]

As discussed briefly above, in *Blue Velvet* the singing voice is just as important as the speaking voice. For the purposes of this case study, I will focus on two voices: those of Dorothy and of Frank. One of the more unusual aspects of the film is Frank's obsession with inhaling helium. This causes his voice to be pitched upward, feminizing it. This feminization of his voice is unusual, given that it occurs in moments when he attempts to overpower or assert dominance over Dorothy. In the script, Lynch writes of the first time that Frank inhales the helium; the gas, Lynch writes, "makes Frank's voice very high and strange sounding. The result is frightening."[35] When the helium's effect runs out, Lynch writes, Frank's voice returns to normal but he returns to take another breath, returning his voice to a high pitch. After this second swig, we obtain a point-of-view sound from Jeffrey's placement in the closet. According to the script: "The high, strange sound reverberates in the distance. Jeffrey can't make it out—soon, he hears Frank's high laughing. … All his breathing—every sound is high."[36] For Lynch, who is obsessed with low sounds, this fixation on high sounds stands out.

On the contrary, Dorothy's voice—specifically, her sultry singing voice—is low, almost masculinized. Chion describes it as "bare, fragile, trembling in the void."[37] Lynch is thus creating a sort of aural role reversal, where the strong, dominant, violent male has a high voice and the helpless, sexualized, female victim has a low voice. This is one example in which Lynch uses the voice to play with the audience's expectations. As David Copenhafer writes about the performance of the title song in the film:

> The diegetic occurrences of *Blue Velvet* are remarkable, however, for being sung by a woman. Interestingly, they are in the same vocal register (Dorothy's version is simply transposed up a whole step, from B-flat to C) as the more famous, recorded version. [Bobby] Vinton's singing shares a kind of androgynous middle ground with Isabella Rossellini's thin yet husky voice.[38]

Lynch has the song transposed downward (likely a necessity due to Rosselini's vocal range and capabilities), but this also has an overall effect on how the song is heard.

Conclusion

When we think about sound design in film, we do not often think about the role of the voice. However, in Lynch's films, the voice plays just as crucial a role as do the sound effects, music, and sound design. Lynch has some typical uses of the voice that can be combined with other techniques, such as dubbing, editing, and volume levels. Vocal ranges of both singing and speaking voices indicate a lot about both character and scene in Lynch's films as do changes in voices. Alterations of vocal range based on the expectations for a particular gender are also important in the director's works in that it defies what the viewer anticipates and alters their interpretation of the character.

Voice can tell us about where and when a character emanates in relation to where they are in the filmic world. Imitations of non-human sounds, including those of animals, also appear frequently in the director's works and indicate primal and often violent characters. This allows the viewer to listen to the voice of the character and immediately guess what kind of role they will play. This is one of the things consistent in Lynch's works that does not defy expectation.

Final Thoughts

As I hope to have shown in this book, Lynch's films have a sonic style all their own, which aids in creating the narratives and structure of the works that are achieved through his vision, collaboration, and sound design techniques. Elements such as sound design, music, and use of the voice are readily recognizable to anyone familiar with the director's works. What makes Lynch's films have such a characteristic sound is his methods of creating sound, not relying on pre-existing sounds but creating them anew.

In his collaborations with composers, he draws on a particular palette of sound, even when describing what he wants through pre-existing pieces of music. His use of pre-existing music, too, has a characteristic sound in that he draws on a particular type of composer, typically Soviet, German, or Polish, specifically in the avant-garde style. Even his use of the voice is characteristic, leaning on screams and timbral effects such as the voice on helium. All of these lend themselves well within films' individual narratives to augment the story through the creation of a sound world.

While there is so much more to discuss regarding Lynch's sonic style, specifically in the context of individual scenes, that I could not mention in a monograph of this length, it is my hope that this book clearly lays out what makes the director's sonic fingerprint identifiable. There is plenty of room to see how these sonic attributes are used in his other filmic works such as his commercials and more recent short films, and I plan to delve into these specifically in future works. In the meantime, I am confident that the reader of this book will become more aware of what makes Lynch's sonic style Lynchian.

Notes

1 Jordan, "Starting from Scratch," 120.
2 Rogers, "The Audiovisual Eerie," 245.
3 Halskov, "'My Dog Barks Some.'"

4 Atkinson, *Blue Velvet*, 56.
5 Phone interview with Dean Hurley, May 21, 2021.
6 Pieter Dom, "Harry Goaz Had His *Twin Peaks* Script Shredded Right After Filming, Says David Bowie Was to Return," *Welcome to Twin Peaks*, May 12, 2016, https://welcometotwinpeaks.com/actors/harry-goaz-new-twin-peaks-script-david-Bowie.
7 Pieter Dom, "Revealed: Actual Twin Peaks Season 3 Script Pages from Part 5 and Part 8 ('Got a Light'?)," *Welcome to Twin Peaks*, May 10, 2018, https://welcometotwinpeaks.com/news/twin-peaks-season-3-script-pages-part-5-part-8/.
8 Smith, "The Auteur Renaissance, 1968–1980," 104.
9 Greene, "The Labour of Breath," 118.
10 Greene, "Bringing Vinyl into The Digital Domain," 105.
11 Van Elferen, "Dream Timbre," 185–86.
12 Morgan, "Darkness Audible," 198.
13 In *Twin Peaks*, the evolution of the arm refers to a being from the Red Room. It is said that when MIKE cut his arm off to rid himself of evil, the arm took on a life of its own, eventually evolving over 25 years into new beings. Murray, "'I Love Winds'" and Rooney, "Air-Object," 139.
14 Ariana DiValentino, "The Screams of Women in Film and What 'Twin Peaks' Can Teach Us About It," *Best Damn Writing*, July 28, 2020, accessed October 28, 2020, https://bestdamnwriting.com/2020/07/28/screaming-hollywood-the-screams-of-women-in-film-and-what-twin-peaks-has-to-say-about-it/.
15 Burt, "'The Thread Will Be Torn'," 114.
16 Rooney, "Air-Object: On Air Media and David Lynch's 'Gotta Light?'" 128.
17 DiValentino, "The Screams of Women in Film."
18 Barrett, "Smashing the Small Screen," 58.
19 Rodley, *Lynch on Lynch*, 166–7.
20 Laura Loguercio Cánepa Correio, Rogério Ferraraz, and Fabiano Pereira de Souza, "O *sound design* de Alan Splet para David Lynch sob a perspectiva do horror fílmico," *Galáxia* 42 (2019): 97–108.
21 Michael Goddard, "Telephones, Voice Recorders, Microphones, Phonographs: A Media Archaeology of Sonic Technologies in *Twin Peaks*," *Senses of Cinema* 79 (2016), http://www.sensesofcinema.com/2016/twin-peaks/sonic-technologies-in-twin-peaks/.
22 Rogers, "The Audiovisual Eerie," 263.
23 McGill, "The Contemporary Hollywood Film Soundtrack," 224–6.
24 Warren Buckland, "The Acousmatic Voice and Metaleptic Narration in *Inland Empire*," in *The Oxford Handbook of Sound and Image in Digital Media*, eds. Carol Vernallis, Amy Herzog, and John Richardson (Oxford and New York: Oxford University Press, 2013), 239.
25 McGill, "The Contemporary Hollywood Film Soundtrack," 238.
26 David Laderman, "(S)lip-Sync: Punk Rock Narrative Film and Postmodern Musical Performance," in *Lowering the Boom: Critical Studies in Film Sound*, eds. Jay Beck and Tony Grajeda (Urbana: University of Illinois Press, 2008), 279.
27 Rogers, "The Audiovisual Eerie," 261.
28 Geneviève Morel, "'This Is the Girl': Note on *Mulholland Drive*, David Lynch (2001)," *in Back to Mulholland Drive: Minimal Fantasy*, ed. Nicolas Bourriaud (Milan: Silviana Editoriale, 2017), 102.
29 Sinnerbrink, "*Silencio*: *Mulholland Drive* as Cinematic Romanticism," 89.
30 McGill, "The Contemporary Hollywood Film Soundtrack," 238.
31 Brooke McCorkle Okazaki, "Where Music Is Always in the Air: Voice and Nostalgia in *Twin Peaks*," in *The Music of Twin Peaks: Listen to the Sounds*, eds. Reba Wissner and Katherine Reed (Abingdon and New York: Routledge, 2021), 49.

32 Reed, "'We Cannot Content Ourselves with Remaining Spectators'," 17.
33 Allister Mactaggart, "'Silencio': Hearing Loss in David Lynch's *Mulholland Drive*," *Journal of Aesthetics & Culture* 6, no. 1 (2014): 4.
34 Sinnerbrink, "*Silencio*," 87.
35 Lynch, *Blue Velvet*, screenplay.
36 Lynch, *Blue Velvet*, screenplay.
37 Chion, *David Lynch*, 43.
38 David Copenhafer, "Mourning and Music in *Blue Velvet*," *Camera Obscura 69* 23, no. 3 (2008): 141.

References

"A Master Class with David Lynch." In *Moviemakers' Master Class: Private Lessons from the World's Foremost Directors*. Edited by Laurent Tirard, 123–34. New York and London: Faber and Faber, 2002.

Alexander, John. *The Films of David Lynch*. London: Charles Letts and Co., 1993.

Alsop, Elizabeth. "'It's No Longer Your Film': Fictions of Authorship in Lynch's *Mulholland Drive*." *Journal of Film and Video* 71, no. 3 (2019): 50–64.

Andersen, Asbjoern. "Behind the Weird, Wonderful Sound of 'Twin Peaks: The Return' –With Dean Hurley and Ron Eng." *A Sound Effect*, October 4, 2017. Accessed February 3, 2019. https://www.asoundeffect.com/twin-peaks-sound/

"Angelo Badalamenti on *Lost Highway*." In *Beyond the Beyond: Music from the Films of David Lynch*. Edited by J. C. Gabel and Jessica Hundley, 93. Los Angeles: Hat and Beard Press, 2016.

Atkinson, Michael. *Blue Velvet (BFI Film Classics)*. London: British Film Institute, 1997.

Barrett, Kyle. "Smashing the Small Screen: David Lynch, *Twin Peaks*, and Reinventing Television." In *Approaching Twin Peaks: Critical Essays on the Original Series*. Edited by Eric Hoffman and Dominic Grace, 47–64. Jefferson, NC: McFarland and Co., 2017.

BBC3. *Sound of Cinema: David Lynch*. May 27, 2023. https://www.bbc.co.uk/sounds/play/m001m569

Bennett, William Weston. "Americana on the Internet: Listening to *Twin Peaks*." In *The Music of Twin Peaks: Listen to the Sounds*. Edited by Reba Wissner and Katherine Reed, 165–80. Abingdon and New York: Routledge, 2021.

Bentley, Jason. "Interview with David Lynch." KCRW Radio, Los Angeles, January 18, 2011. Accessed February 3, 2019. https://www.kcrw.com/music/shows/morning-beomes-eclectic/david-lynch/

Bobée, Emmanuelle. "Monde 'réel' et monde imaginaire. Le rôle de la bande son dans *Eraserhead*, de David Lynch." *Entrelacs* 8 (2011). Accessed December 1, 2018. https://journals.openedition.org/entrelacs/236

Buckland, Warren. "The Acousmatic Voice and Metaleptic Narration in *Inland Empire*." In *The Oxford Handbook of Sound and Image in Digital Media*. Edited by Carol Vernallis, Amy Herzog, and John Richardson, 236–49. Oxford and New York: Oxford University Press, 2013.

Burt, Andrew T. "Is It the Wind in the Tall Trees or Just the Distant Buzz of Electricity? Sound and Music as Portent in *Twin Peaks'* Season Three." In *Critical Essays on*

Twin Peaks: The Return. Edited by Antonio Sanna, 253–58. New York: Palgrave Macmillan, 2019.

———. "'The Thread Will Be Torn': Sound Design as a Measure of Self-Knowledge in *Twin Peaks: Fire Walk With Me*." In *The Music of Twin Peaks: Listen to the Sounds*. Edited by Reba Wissner and Katherine Reed, 107–20. Abington and New York: Routledge, 2021.

Bushman, David. *Conversations with Mark Frost: Twin Peaks, Hill Street Blues, and the Education of a Writer*. Columbus, OH: Fayetteville Mafia Press, 2020.

Channel 4 Television London. "Angelo Badalamenti On His Career." *Channel 4 Television Online* (London). Accessed June 7, 2021. http://www.channel4.com/film/reviews/feature.jsp?id=111752

Chen, Min. "How *Twin Peaks* Got Its Super Creepy Sound." *Surface*, September 15, 2017. Accessed September 28, 2018. https://www.surfacemag.com/articles/dean-hurley-on-twin-peaks-anthology-resource-vol-1/

Chion, Michel. *David Lynch*. trans. Robert Julian. London: British Film Institute, 1995.

———. *David Lynch*. 2nd edition, trans. Robert Julian. London: British Film Institute, 2006.

———. "The Silence of the Loudspeaker, or Why with the Dolby Sound It Is the Sound that Listens to Us," April 16, 1998. In *Soundscape: The School of Sound Lectures*, 1998–2001. Edited by Larry Sider, Diane Freeman, and Jerry Sider, 150–54. London and New York: Wallflower Press, 2003.

Ciment, Michel and Hubert Niogret. "Interview with David Lynch" (1990). In *David Lynch: Interviews*. Edited by Richard A. Barney, 106–24. Jackson: University Press of Mississippi, 2009.

Copenhafer, David. "Mourning and Music in *Blue Velvet*." *Camera Obscura* 23, no. 3 (2008): 136–57.

Correio, Laura Loguercio Cánepa, Rogério Ferraraz, and Fabiano Pereira de Souza. "O *sound design* de Alan Splet para David Lynch sob a perspectiva do horror fílmico." *Galáxia* 42 (2019): 96–108.

David Lynch Teaches Creativity and Film. "Sound Design and Scoring." *Masterclass*, May 2019. https://www.masterclass.com/classes/david-lynch-teaches-creativity-and-film/chapters/sound-design-and-scoring

David Lynch Theater. *YouTube*. Accessed September 14, 2020. https://www.youtube.com/c/DAVIDLYNCHTHEATER/videos

Davison, Annette. "Demystified, Remystified, and Seduced by Sirens: Listening to David Lynch's Films." In *Essays on Sound and Vision*. Edited by John Richardson and Stan Hawkins, 119–54. Yliopistopaino: Helsinki University Press, 2007.

———. "'Up in Flames': Love, Control, and Collaboration in the Soundtrack to *Wild at Heart*." In *The Cinema of David Lynch: American Dreams, Nightmare Visions*. Edited by Erica Sheen and Annette Davison, 119–35. London and New York: Wallflower Press, 2004.

Di Rosso, Jason. "Dean Hurley is David Lynch's Long Time Sound and Music Collaborator." *The Screen Show*. Australian Broadcasting Company, November 15, 2018. Accessed February 15, 2019. https://abcmedia.akamaized.net/rn/podcast/2018/11/sch_20181115_1020.mp3

Dieringer, Jon. "The Frequency of Fear: Dean Hurley Interview." *Screen Slate*, December 7, 2018. https://www.screenslate.com/articles/frequency-fear-dean-hurley-interview

DiValentino, Ariana. "The Screams of Women in Film and What 'Twin Peaks' Can Teach Us About It." *Best Damn Writing*, July 28, 2020. Accessed October 28, 2020. https://bestdamnwriting.com/2020/07/28/screaming-hollywood-the-screams-of-women-in-film-and-what-twin-peaks-has-to-say-about-it/

Dom, Pieter. "Harry Goaz Had His *Twin Peaks Script Shredded Right After Filming, Says David Bowie* Was to Return." *Welcome to Twin Peaks*, May 12, 2016. https://welcometotwinpeaks.com/actors/harry-goaz-new-twin-peaks-script-david-Bowie

———. "Revealed: Actual Twin Peaks Season 3 Script Pages from Part 5 and Part 8 ('Got a Light'?)." *Welcome to Twin Peaks*, May 10, 2018. https://welcometotwinpeaks.com/news/twin-peaks-season-3-script-pages-part-5-part-8/

Donnelly, K. J. *The Spectre of Sound: Music in Film and Television*. New York and London: Bloomsbury, 2019.

Douridas, Chris. "Interview (1997)". In *David Lynch: Interviews*. Edited by Richard A. Barney, 150–62. Jackson: University Press of Mississippi, 2009.

Eyes on Cinema. *Master of Sound: Alan Splet: Interviews with Peter Weir and David Lynch*. YouTube, 10:58, March 15, 2015. Accessed January 12, 2019. https://www.youtube.com/watch?v=Y0-HCecz8FQ/

Farley, Shaun. "Ann Kroeber Special: BBC Interview." *Designing Sound*, October 25, 2011. Accessed February 28, 2011. http://designingsound.org/2011/10/25/ann-kroeber-special-bbc-interview/

Frank, Josh. *In Heaven Everything is Fine: The Unsolved Life of Peter Ivers and the Lost History of New Wave Theatre*. New York: Free Press, 2008.

Gentry, Ric. "Alan Splet and Sound Effects for *Dune*." *American Cinematographer* (December 1984): 62–72.

George, Kenneth. *Dune: The David Lynch Files: Volume 2*. Orlando: Bear Manor Media, 2020.

Getman, Jessica. "Playing with Sound: Fan Engagement with the Soundtrack of *Twin Peaks: The Return* (2017)." In *The Music of Twin Peaks: Listen to the Sounds*. Edited by Reba Wissner and Katherine Reed, 34–47. Abingdon and New York: Routledge, 2021.

Giannopolou, Zina. "Introduction." In *Mulholland Drive*. Edited by Zina Giannopolou, 1–7. London and New York: Routledge, 2013.

Givens, Ron. "Creative Contrasts: Making Moody Music." *Entertainment Weekly*, April 6, 1990. http://www.ew.com/ew/article/0,,317090,00.html

Goddard, Michael. "Telephones, Voice Recorders, Microphones, Phonographs: A Media Archaeology of Sonic Technologies in *Twin Peaks*." *Senses of Cinema* 79 (2016). http://www.sensesofcinema.com/2016/twin-peaks/sonic-technologies-in-twin-peaks/

Godwin, K. George. "*Eraserhead* by David Lynch." *Film Quarterly* 39, no. 1 (1985): 37.

Godwin, Kenneth George. "Interview with David Lynch, December 1981." In *Eraserhead: The David Lynch Files: Volume 1*. Edited by Kenneth George Godwin, 131–260. Orlando: Bear Manor Media, 2020.

Greene, Liz. "Bringing Vinyl into The Digital Domain: Aesthetics in David Lynch's *Inland Empire* (2006)." *The New Soundtrack* 2, no. 2 (2012): 97–111.

———. "The Elephant Man's Sound, Tracked." April 30, 2020. http://www.vimeo.com/413827977

———. "From Noise: Blurring the Boundaries of the Soundtrack." In *The Palgrave Handbook of Sound Design and Music*. Edited by Liz Greene and Danijela Kulezic-Wilson, 17–32. New York: Palgrave Macmillan, 2016.

———. "Interview 1: Sound Recording, Sound Design, and Collaboration—An Interview with Ann Kroeber." In *The Palgrave Handbook of Sound Design and Music*. Edited by Liz Greene and Danijela Kulezic-Wilson, 33–42. New York: Palgrave Macmillan, 2016.

———. "The Labour of Breath: Performing and Designing Breath in Cinema." *Music, Sound, and the Moving Image* 10, no. 2 (2016): 109–33.

———. "Speaking, Singing, Screaming: Controlling the Female Voice in American Cinema." *The Soundtrack* 2, no. 1 (2009): 1–15.

Griffiths, Emma. "Q&A with David Lynch's Music Collaborator Dean Hurley – Part 1: Working On and 'Protecting The Experience' of *Twin Peaks: The Return*." *Synchtank*, July 21, 2017. Accessed July 30, 2018. https://www.synchtank.com/blog/qa-with-david-lynchs-music-collaborator-dean-hurley-part-1-working-on-and-protecting-the-experience-of-twin-peaks-the-return/

Grønstad, Asbjø Skarsvåg. *Rethinking Art and Visual Culture: The Poetics of Opacity*. Springer International Publishing AG, 2020.

Hageman, Andrew. "The Uncanny Ecology of *Mulholland Drive*." In *Back to Mulholland Drive: Minimal Fantasy*. Edited by Nicolas Bourriaud, 140–67. Milan: Silviana Editoriale, 2017.

Hainge, Greg. *Noise Matters: Towards an Ontology of Noise*. New York and London: Bloomsbury, 2013.

———. "Weird or Loopy? Specular Spaces, Feedback and Artifice in *Lost Highway*'s Aesthetics of Sensation." In *The Cinema of David Lynch: American Dreams, Nightmare Visions*. Edited by Erica Sheen and Annette Davison, 136–50. London and New York: Wallflower Press, 2004.

Halsall, Philip. *The Films of David Lynch: 50 Percent Sound*. London: British Film Resource, 2002. Accessed October 2, 2018. http://www.britishfilm.org.uk/lynch/Sintro.html

Halskov, Andreas. "'My Dog Barks Some': Animalistic Sounds and Motifs in the Works of David Lynch." *25 Years Later Site*, October 20, 2017. Accessed September 15, 2018. https://25yearslatersite.com/2017/10/20/my-dog-barks-some-animalistic-sounds-and-motifs-in-the-works-of-david-lynch/

Hartmann, Mike. "Lost in Darkness and Confusion." *The City of Absurdity: The Mysterious World of David Lynch*. Accessed June 7, 2021. http://www.thecityofabsurdity.com/

Hayward, Philip. "Introduction: Scoring the Edge." In *Terror Tracks: Music, Sound, and Horror Media*. Edited by Philip Hayward, 1–13. London and Oakville: Equinox Publishing, 2009.

Hewitt, Tim. "Is There Life After *Dune*? (1986)." In *David Lynch: Interviews*. Edited by Richard A. Barney, 29–33. Jackson: University Press of Mississippi, 2009.

Hope, Cat. "The Bottom End of Cinema: Low Frequency Effects in Soundtrack Composition." In *Sound Scripts: Proceedings of the 2007 Totally Huge New Music Festival*. Volume 2. Edited by Cat Hope and Jonathan W. Marshall, 74–78. Sydney: Australian Music Centre, 2009.

Hughes, David. *The Complete Lynch*. London: Virgin Publishing, 2001.

Indiana, Gary. "Good Eraserhead: Indiana" (1980). In *David Lynch: Interviews*. Edited by Richard A. Barney, 9–18. Jackson: University Press of Mississippi, 2009.

"Interview with Alan Splet." *Cagey Films*, December 17, 1981. Accessed March 1, 2019. https://web.archive.org/web/20121201060512/http:/www.cageyfilms.com/links/eraserhead/interviews/other-eraserhead-crew/alan-splet/

Jordan, Randolph. "Starting from Scratch: Turntables, Auditory Representation, and the Structure of the Known Universe in the Films of David Lynch." MA Thesis, Concordia University, Canada, 2003.

Joyce, Colin. "This is Why the New 'Twin Peaks' Sounds as Weird as Shit." *Noisey .com*, August 18, 2017. Accessed October 9, 2018. https://noisey.vice.com/en_us/article/wjjxe9/this-is-why-the-new-twin-peaks-sounds-weird-as-shit/

Kaleta, Kenneth C. *David Lynch*. New York: Twayne Publishers, 1992.

Kenny, Tom. *Sound for Picture: Film Sound Through the 1990s*. Vallejo, CA: Mix Books, 2000.

KEXP. "How David Lynch Fell in Love with Au Revoir Simone." *KEXP Soundcloud*, 2018. https://soundcloud.com/kexp/how-david-lynch-fell-in-love

KEXP. "Twin Peaks: Who Signs that Cool Version of Viva Las Vegas?" July 24, 2017. https://soundcloud.com/kexp/twin-peaks-who-signs-that-cool-version-of-viva-las-vegas

Klein, Andy. "Director's Notes." *The Hollywood Reporter*, Film & TV Music Special Issue, 1990. Accessed December 12, 2018. http://www.thecityofabsurdity.com/intmusic.html

Kohler, Andrew S. "'Like Some Haunting Melody': The Laura Palmer Theme in the World of *Twin* Peaks." In *The Music of Twin Peaks: Listen to the Sounds*. Edited by Reba Wissner and Katherine Reed, 181–202. Abingdon and New York: Routledge, 2021.

Kulezic-Wilson, Danijela. *The Musicality of Narrative Film*. Houndsmills and Basingstoke: Palgrave Macmillan, 2015.

———. *Sound Design is the New Score: Theory, Aesthetics, and Erotics of the Integrated Soundtrack*. Oxford and New York: Oxford University Press, 2020.

Laderman, David. "(S)lip-Sync: Punk Rock Narrative Film and Postmodern Musical Performance." In *Lowering the Boom: Critical Studies in Film Sound*. Edited by Jay Beck and Tony Grajeda, 269–87. Urbana: University of Illinois Press, 2008.

Lehman, Frank. "Optigan Illusions: Sonic Dislocation in *The Return*." *Musicology Now*, December 20, 2017. https://musicologynow.org/optigan-allusions-sonic-dislocation-in-the-return/

Lim, Dennis. *David Lynch: The Man from Another Place*. New York: Amazon Publishing, 2015.

Lloyd, Rose. "Tumoresque: The Films of David Lynch." *Atlantic* (October 1984): 108. https://www.theatlantic.com/magazine/archive/1984/10/tumoresque-the-films-of-david-lynch/664964/

Lombardo, Patrizia. *Memory and Imagination in Film: Scorsese, Lynch, Jarmusch, Van Sant*. New York: Palgrave Macmillan, 2014.

"Love, Death, Elvis & Oz: The Making of 'Wild at Heart.'" DVD, *Wild at Heart*, 2004.

Lynch, David. "Action and Reaction," April 17, 1998. In *Soundscape: The School of Sound Lectures, 1998–2001*. Edited by Larry Sider, Diane Freeman, and Jerry Sider, 49–53. London and New York: Wallflower Press, 2003.

———. *The Art Life*. DVD.

———. *Blue Velvet.* Undated Script. Accessed January 3, 2019. http://www.lynchnet.com/bv/bvscript.html

———. *Catching the Big Fish: Meditation, Consciousness, and Creativity.* 10th anniversary edition. New York: TarcherPerigee, 2016.

———. *Lost Highway.* Script, June 21, 1995. Accessed March 1, 2019. http://www.lynchnet.com/lh/lhscript.html

———. *The Marriage of Picture and Sound,* audio CD, track 3, "The Marriage of Picture and Sound." Nürnberg: Moderne Kunst Nürnberg, 2012.

———. *Wild at Heart.* Screenplay, 1990. https://assets.scriptslug.com/live/pdf/scripts/wild-at-heart-1990.pdf

Lynch, David and Kristine McKenna. *Room to Dream.* New York: Random House, 2018.

Macfehin, Laura. "Music Supervisor Dean Hurley Talks *Twin Peaks.*" *UndertheRadar.com,* August 31, 2017. Accessed February 9, 2019. https://www.undertheradar.co.nz/interview/913/Music-Supervisor-Dean-Hurley-Talks-Twin-Peaks.utr

Machlin, Paul S. *Stride: The Music of Fats Waller.* London: MacMillan Press, 1985.

Mactaggart, Allister. "'I Am Dead, Yet I Live': Revealing the Enigma of Art in *Twin Peaks*: The Return." *NANO: New American Notes Online* 15 (2020). https://nanocrit.com/issues/issue15/I-am-dead-yet-I-live-Revealing-the-Enigma-of-Art-in-Twin-Peaks-The-Return

———. "'Silencio': Hearing Loss in David Lynch's *Mulholland Drive.*" *Journal of Aesthetics & Culture* 6, no. 1 (2014): 1–11.

Malavasi, Luca. *Mulholland Drive.* Turin: Lindau, 2008.

Marshall, Colin. "What David Lynch Can Do with a 100-Year-Old Camera and 52 Seconds of Film." *Open Culture,* May 9, 2012. Accessed November 2, 2018. http://www.openculture.com/2012/05/what_david_lynch_can_do_with_a_100-year-old_camera_and_52_seconds_of_film.html/

Marshall, Kingsley and Rupert Loydell. "'Listen to the Sounds': Sound and Storytelling in *Twin Peaks: The Return.*" In *Critical Essays on Twin Peaks: The Return.* Edited by Antonio Sanna, 269–80. New York: Palgrave Macmillan, 2019.

———. "Sound Design, Music, and the Birth of Evil in *Twin Peaks: The* Return." In *The Music of Twin Peaks: Listen to the Sounds.* Edited by Reba Wissner and Katherine Reed, 121–34. Abingdon and New York: Routledge, 2021.

Martin, Richard. "Neighborhoods or Nothing? Social Relations in David Lynch's *Blue Velvet.*" *European Journal of American Culture* 32, no. 3 (2013): 235–47.

Mattarelli, Ricardo Sampino. *David Lynch: Sound Designer.* Falconara Mattima: Edizioni Crac, 2014.

Mazullo, Mark. "Remembering Pop: David Lynch and the Sound of the '60s." *American Music* 23, no. 4 (2005): 493–513.

McCorkle, Brooke. "There's Always Music in the Air: Sound Design in *Twin Peaks: The Return.*" *Musicology Now,* December 12, 2017. Accessed October 27, 2020. http://www.musicologynow.org/2017/12/theres-always-music-in-air-sound-design.html

McGill, Amy Charlotte. "The Contemporary Hollywood Film Soundtrack: Professional Practices and Sonic Styles Since the 1970s." Ph.D. Dissertation, University of Exeter, 2008.

McGowan, Todd. *The Impossible David Lynch.* New York: Columbia University Press, 2007.

McKibbin, Tony. "Listening to Lynch." *Film Ireland* 115 (2007): np.

Miley, Mike. "David Lynch at the Crossroads: Deconstructing Rock, Reconstructing *Wild at Heart*." *Music and the Moving Image* 7, no. 3 (2014): 41–60.

"The Monster Meets...Filmmaker David Lynch." *The Home Theater Buyers Guide* (Fall 1998). Accessed March 1, 2019. http://www.lynchnet.com/monster.html

Morel, Geneviève, "'This is the Girl': Note on *Mulholland Drive*, David Lynch (2001)." In *Back to Mulholland Drive: Minimal Fantasy*. Edited by Nicolas Bourriaud, 94–107. Milan: Silviana Editoriale, 2017.

Morgan, Frances. "'A Beautiful Trip': An Interview with David Lynch." *The Quietus*, December 12, 2011. Accessed March 1, 2019. https://thequietus.com/articles/07565-david-lynch-interview

———. "Darkness Audible: Sub-Bass, Tape Decay and Lynchian Noise." In *The End: An Electric Sheep Anthology*. Edited by Virginia Selavy, 186–202. London: Strange Attractor Press, 2011.

Murray, Noel. "'I Love Winds': David Lynch on the Sound of 'Twin Peaks.'" *The New York Times*, August 17, 2017. Accessed October 2, 2018. https://www.nytimes.com/2017/08/17/arts/television/david-lynch-twin-peaks-interview.html/

———. "Subverting the Classic Score: *The Elephant Man/Dune/The Straight Story*." In *Beyond the Beyond: Music from the Films of David Lynch*. Edited by J.C. Gabel and Jessica Hundley, 75–84. Los Angeles: Hat and Beard Press, 2016.

Mysteries of Love: The Making of Blue Velvet. DVD, *Blue Velvet*, 2002.

Naha, Ed. *The Making of Dune*. New York: Berkeley Books, 1984.

Ness, Richard R. "A Lotta Night Music: The Sound of *Film Noir*." *Cinema Journal* 47, no. 2 (2008): 52–73.

Nochimson, Martha P. *David Lynch Swerves: Uncertainty from Lost Highway to Inland Empire*. Austin: University of Texas Press, 2014.

———. *The Passion of David Lynch: Wild at Heart in Hollywood*. Austin: University of Texas Press, 2012.

———. *Television Rewired: The Rise of the Auteur Series*. Austin: University of Texas Press, 2019.

Norelli, Clare Nina. *Soundtrack from Twin Peaks*. New York: Bloomsbury, 2017.

———. "Suburban Dread: The Music of Angelo Badalamenti in the Films of David Lynch." In *Sound Scripts: Proceedings of the 2007 Totally Huge New Music Festival*. Volume 2. Edited by Cat Hope and Jonathan W. Marshall, 38–43. New South Wales: Australian Music Centre, 2009.

Odell, Colin and Michelle LeBlanc. *David Lynch*. Harpender: Kamera Books, 2007.

O'Falt, Chris. "Sound Comes First: Inside David Lynch's Bunker, Where He Started Creating the 'Twin Peaks' Sound Design Over 7 Years Ago." *IndieWire*, May 17, 2018. Accessed October 2, 2018. https://www.indiewire.com/2018/05/twin-peaks-the-return-sound-design-david-lynch-hidden-studio-process-dean-hurley-1201965234/

Okazaki, Brooke McCorkle. "Where Music is Always in the Air: Voice and Nostalgia in *Twin Peaks*." In *The Music of Twin Peaks: Listen to the Sounds*. Edited by Reba Wissner and Katherine Reed, 48–62. Abingdon and New York: Routledge, 2021.

Olson, Greg. *David Lynch: Beautiful Dark*. Lanham, MD and Toronto: Scarecrow Press, 2008.

Osborn, Brad. "The Subdominant Tritone in Film and Television Music." *Current Musicology* 107 (2020): 62–92.

Phillips, Lior. "Lykke Li and Dean Hurley Explain What 'Lynchian' Means: David Lynch's Past Collaborators Pull Aside The Red Velvet Curtains." *Consequence of Sound*, September 2, 2017. Accessed October 3, 2018. https://consequenceofsound.net/2017/09/lykke-li-and-dean-hurley-explain-what-lynchian-means/

Phipps, Keith. "Industrial Soundscapes: *Eraserhead/Lost Highway/Inland Empire*." In *Beyond the Beyond: Music from the Films of David Lynch*. Edited by J. C. Gabel and Jessica Hundley, 85–96. Los Angeles: Hat and Beard Press, 2016.

Power, Dominic. "'This Is a Story That Happened Yesterday but I Know It's Tomorrow': David Lynch's *Inland Empire*." *The Soundtrack* 1, no. 1 (2007): 53–55.

Ray, Kate. *Ominous Whoosh* (@OminousWhoosh). https://twitter.com/ominouswhoosh?lang=en

Reed, Katherine. "The Bang Bang Bar, Silencio, and Lynch's Audiences: Meaning and Musical Performances in *Twin Peaks: The Return*." In *The Music of Twin Peaks: Listen to the Sounds*. Edited by Reba Wissner and Katherine Reed, 63–76. Abingdon and New York: Routledge, 2021.

———. "'We Cannot Content Ourselves with Remaining Spectators': Musical Performance, Audience Interaction, and Nostalgia in the Films of David Lynch." *Music and the Moving Image* 9, no. 1 (2016): 3–22.

Reid, James D. and Candace R. Craig. *Agency and Imagination in the Films of David Lynch: Philosophical Perspectives*. Lanham, MD: Lexington Books, 2019.

Richardson, John. "*Laura* and *Twin Peaks*: Postmodern Parody and the Musical Reconstruction of the Absent Femme Fatale." In *The Cinema of David Lynch: American Dreams, Nightmare Visions*. Edited by Erica Sheen and Annette Davison, 77–92. London: Wallflower Press, 2004.

Riggott, Julie. "New Music Shines in the Projector's Beam." *USC Thornton School of Music*, April 9, 2015. Accessed September 14, 2020. https://music.usc.edu/new-music-shines-in-the-projectors-beam/

Robertson, Robert. *Cinema and the Audiovisual Imagination: Music, Image, Sound*. London and New York: I. B. Taurus, 2015.

Robinson, Joanna. "Twin Peaks: 20 Easter Eggs, References, and Callbacks You Might Have Missed." *Vanity Fair*, May 23, 2017. https://www.vanityfair.com/hollywood/2017/05/twin-peaks-season-1-easter-eggs-episode-1-2-3-4

Rodley, Chris. "The *Icon* Profile: David Lynch (1997)." In *David Lynch: Interviews*. Edited by Richard A. Barney, 180–93. Jackson: University Press of Mississippi, 2009.

———, ed. *Lynch on Lynch*, rev. ed. London: Faber and Faber, 1997.

Rodman, Ron. *Tuning In: American Narrative Television Music*. Oxford and New York: Oxford University Press, 2010.

Rogers, Holly. "The Audiovisual Eerie: Transmediating Thresholds in the Work of David Lynch." In *Transmedia Directors: Artistry, Industry and the New Audiovisual Aesthetics*. Edited by Carol Vernalis, Holly Rogers, and Lisa Perrott, 241–70. New York: Bloomsbury, 2019.

Rooney, Monique. "Air-Object: On Air Media and David Lynch's 'Gotta Light?' (*Twin Peaks: The Return*, 2017)." *New Review of Film and Television Studies* 16, no. 2 (2018): 123–43.

Ruimy, Jordan. "David Lynch: 'If You're Playing a Move on A Phone, You Will Never in a Trillion Years Experience The Film.'" *World of Reel*, December 30, 2019. https://www.worldofreel.com/blog/2019/12/flashback-david-lynch

Saban, Stephen and Sarah Longacre. "Eraserhead: Is There Life After Birth?" (1977). In *David Lynch: Interviews*. Edited by Richard A. Barney, 3–8. Jackson: University Press of Mississippi, 2009.

Samardzija, Zoran. "DavidLynch.com: Auteurship in the Age of the Internet and Digital Cinema." *Scope* 16 (2012). Accessed February 12, 2019. https://www.nottingham.ac.uk/scope/documents/2010/february-2010/samardzija.pdf

Samuels, Stuart. *Midnight Movies*. New York: Collier Books, 1983.

Sanger, Jonathan. *Making The Elephant Man: A Producer's Memoir*. Jefferson, NC: McFarland and Co., 2016.

Schulenberg, Martha. "The Music is Not What It Seems: An Examination of Labor and Capital in the Music of *Twin Peaks: The Return* Series." In *The Music of Twin Peaks: Listen to the Sounds*. Edited by Reba Wissner and Katherine Reed, 77–90. Abingdon and New York: Routledge, 2021.

Schweiger, Daniel. "The Madman and His Muse." *Film Score Monthly* (September 2001): 24–27, 44.

Siegel, Ira. Keynote roundtable panelist. "Recording Session Musicians in New York City." Music and the Moving Image conference, New York University, May, 28, 2021.

Simonini, Ross. "'Daydreaming Is So Important to Me': How David Lynch Fishes For Ideas." *Art Review*, January 25, 2021. https://artreview.com/daydreaming-is-so-important-to-me-how-david-lynch-fishes-for-ideas/

Sinnerbrink, Robert. "*Silencio*: *Mulholland Drive* as Cinematic Romanticism." In *Mulholland Drive*. Edited by Zina Giannopolou, 75–96. London and New York: Routledge, 2013.

Smaczylo, Mike. "David Lynch and the Surreal Soundscapes of Mulholland Drive." *Muse by Clio*, April 28, 2020. https://musebycl.io/music-film/david-lynch-and-surreal-soundscapes-mulholland-drive

Smith, Jeff. "The Auteur Renaissance, 1968–1980." In *Sound: Dialogue, Music, and Effects*. Edited by Kathryn Kalinak, 83–106. New Brunswick, NJ: Rutgers University Press, 2015.

Smith, Murray. "Theses on the Philosophy of Hollywood History." In *Contemporary Hollywood Cinema*. Edited by Steve Neale and Murray Smith, 3–20. London: Routledge, 1998.

Special to *Studio Daily*. "Sound Designer Randy Thom on a Career in Film Sound." *Studio Daily*, January 24, 2014. Accessed March 2, 2019. http://www.studiodaily.com/2014/01/sound-designer-randy-thom-on-a-career-in-film-sound/

Stilwell, Robynn J. "The Fantastical Gap between Diegetic and Nondiegetic." In *Beyond the Soundtrack: Representing Music in Cinema*. Edited by Daniel Goldmark, Lawrence Kramer, and Richard Leppert, 184–202. Berkeley and Los Angeles: University of California Press, 2007.

TheJunkBucket. "Mulholland Drive: Behind the Scenes." YouTube, December 3, 2017. https://www.youtube.com/watch?v=Ik0vi0Qm5ts

The Paris Review. "David Lynch on Alan Splet." YouTube, 12:57, May 13, 2014. Accessed January 2, 2019. https://www.theparisreview.org/blog/2014/05/13/snapping-humming-buzzing-banging-remembering-alan-splet/

Thom, Randy. "Designing a Movie for Sound, April 17, 1988." In *Soundscape: The School of Sound Lectures, 1998–2001*. Edited by Larry Sider, Diane Freeman, and Jerry Sider, 121–37. London and New York: Wallflower Press, 2003.

Toles, George. *Curtains of Light: Theatrical Space in Film*. Albany: SUNY Press, 2021.

Toraman, Zeynep. "What is Gordon Cole Listening To? The Rhetoric of Subjective Sound in *Twin Peaks: The Return*." In *The Music of Twin Peaks: Listen to the Sounds*. Edited by Reba Wissner and Katherine Reed, 135–48. Abingdon and New York: Routledge, 2021.

"*Twin Peaks*: An Interview with Music Director Dean Hurley." *Rhino.com*, August 11, 2017. Accessed June 1, 2018. https://www.rhino.com/article/twin-peaks-an-interview-with-music-director-dean-hurley

Van Elferen, Isabella. "Dream Timbre: Notes on Lynchian Sound Design." In *Music, Sound, and Filmmakers: Sonic Style in Cinema*. Edited by James Wierzbicki, 175–88. New York and Abingdon: Routledge, 2012.

Vest, Lisa Cooper. *Awangarda: Tradition and Modernity in Postwar Polish Music*. Berkeley and Los Angeles: University of California Press, 2020.

Virginás, Andrea. "Television and Video Screens in Filmic Narratives: Medium Specificity, Noise, and Frame-Work." *Acta Universitatis Sapentiae, Film and Media Studies* 17 (2019): 81–96.

von Stosch, Alexandra. "The Story of Time and Space Concepts—Of Reality in the Work of John Cage and David Lynch." In *David Lynch: The Art of the Real*, Conference Proceedings, Braunschweig, 2016. Edited by Thomas Becker, Wolfram Bergande, Alexandra v. Stosch, and Valeska Schmidt-Thomsen. Accessed January 26, 2019. http://lynchconference.hbk-bs.de/the-story-of-time-and-space-concepts-of-reality-in-the-work-of-john-cage-and-david-lynch/

Wallace, David Foster. "David Lynch Keeps His Head." In *A Supposedly Fun Thing I'll Never Do Again: Essays and Arguments*, 147–212. New York: Little, Brown, and Co., 1997.

Walter, Brian. "Wild Things: Music and Masculinity in *Something Wild* and *Blue Velvet*." *Music, Sound and the Moving Image* 6, no. 2 (2012): 163–83.

Webb, Daisy. "In Heaven: Celebrating the Surreal Sounds of David Lynch." *Film Daily*. Accessed March 1, 2019. https://filmdaily.co/obsessions/the-surreal-sounds-david-lynch/

West, Kai. "Listen to the Skins: Drumming and Time in *Twin Peaks*." In *The Music of Twin Peaks: Listen to the Sounds*. Edited by Reba Wissner and Katherine Reed, 203–17. Abingdon and New York: Routledge, 2021.

Willemsen, Steven and Miklos Kiss. "Last Year at Mulholland Drive: Ambiguous Framings and Framing Ambiguities." *Acta Universitatis Sapentiae, Film and Media Studies* 16 (2019): 129–52.

Willet, Eugene Kenneth Willet. "Music as *Sinthome*: Joy Riding with Lacan, Lynch, and Beethoven Beyond Postmodernism." Ph.D. Dissertation, University of Texas at Austin, 2007.

Wilson, Scott. "Neuracinema." In *David Lynch in Theory*. Edited by François-Xavier Gleyzon, 415–19. Prague: Univerzita Karlova v Praze, 2010.

Wilson, Steven. "David Lynch's Metaphysical Sound Design: The Acousmatic Personification of Judy." In *The Music of Twin Peaks: Listen to the Sounds*. Edited by Reba Wissner and Katherine Reed, 149–62. Abingdon and New York: Routledge, 2021.

Winters, Ben. "Musical Wallpaper? Towards an Appreciation of Non-Narrating Music in Film." *Music, Sound, and the Moving Image* 6, no. 1 (2012): 39–54.

Wissner, Reba. "Isn't It too Dreamy? Music and Nostalgia in *The Return*." *25 Years Later Site*, December 10, 2017. https://25yearslatersite.com/2017/12/10/isnt-it-too-dreamy-music-and-nostalgia-in-the-return/

———. "Krzysztof Penderecki's *Threnody for the Victims of Hiroshima* and the Trinity Atomic Bomb Test in *Twin Peaks: The Return*." *Musicology Now*, December 21, 2017. Accessed October 27, 2020. http://www.musicologynow.org/2017/12/krzysztof-pendereckis-threnody-for.html

Wissner, Reba and Katherine Reed, eds. *The Music of Twin Peaks: Listen to the Sounds*. Abingdon and New York: Routledge, 2021.

Woods, Paul A. *Weirdsville USA: The Obsessive Universe of David Lynch*. London: Plexus Publishing, 2000.

Woodward, Richard B. "Snapping, Humming, Buzzing, Banging: Remembering Alan Splet." *The Paris Review*, May 13, 2014. Accessed October 1, 2018. https://www.theparisreview.org/blog/2014/05/13/snapping-humming-buzzing-banging-remembering-alan-splet/

Wray, Daniel Dylan. "The Secrets Behind the Music of 'Twin Peaks: The Return.'" *Pitchfork*, September 4, 2017. https://pitchfork.com/features/article/the-secrets-behind-the-music-of-twin-peaks-the-return/

Žižek, Slavoj. *The Art of the Ridiculous Sublime: On David Lynch's Lost Highway*. Seattle: Walter Chapin Simpson Center for the Humanities, 2000.

Index

For Product Safety Concerns and Information please contact our EU representative GPSR@taylorandfrancis.com
Taylor & Francis Verlag GmbH, Kaufingerstraße 24, 80331 München, Germany

www.ingramcontent.com/pod-product-compliance
Lightning Source LLC
LaVergne TN
LVHW010932110826
845149LV00013B/2562

* 9 7 8 1 0 3 2 2 0 8 3 5 0 *